CHILDREN'S PARTY CAKES

CHILDREN'S PARTY CAKES

50 IMAGINATIVE STEP-BY-STEP RECIPES

CAROLE HANDSLIP

TED SMART

To my family, Simon, Nicholas and Susanna, who thought up
all the designs and gobbled down all the cake.

Published in 1991 by Ebury Press
an imprint of the Random Century Group
Random Century House
20 Vauxhall Bridge Road
London SW1V 2SA

British Library Cataloguing-In-Publication Data
Handslip, Carole
Children's party cakes.
I. Title
641.8

ISBN 0–7126–4714–7 (hardback)
ISBN 0–09–175172–1 (paperback)

Editor: Barbara Croxford
Photographer: Ferguson Hill
Designer: Peartree Design Associates

Typeset in Gill Sans by Textype Typesetters, Cambridge
Printed and bound in Italy by New Interlitho S.p.a., Milan

CONTENTS

INTRODUCTION

I have always enjoyed icing cakes for my children each year on their birthdays. On these occasions my husband and I will be found in the kitchen late at night, with sticky fingers and faces, surrounded by cake crumbs, sweets and various coloured icings; tired but happy and hoping that all our efforts will be worthwhile.

The next morning, when the children come down to see a teddy bear, a sailing boat or a space ship sitting on the kitchen table, the excitement and wonder on their faces is all the reward we need.

It really is great fun if you and your partner both help with the decorating; ideas always flow better with two working together. One will suddenly remember that sailing boats have lifebelts, so out come the Polos. Wouldn't it be better if teddy had claws? – so liquorice is put to good use. Ideas pour out as you see the cake taking shape.

Don't be put off if you are short of time or talent – many of the designs simply call for assembly and finishing, using bought cakes. Not even the chocolate coating is always necessary – the train, for instance, would be quite effective without coating.

Some of the cakes require more patience and attention to detail. Designs like Concorde, grand piano and snooker table are quite fiddly and time consuming but worth the trouble, especially if your child is an enthusiast on the subject. It just wouldn't do to have incorrectly coloured snooker balls, a piano without both black and white keys, or a Concorde with a stuck up nose.

I was assailed with roars of laughter when my family saw the sailing boat, apparently the sails were not attached to the forestay (whatever that is!), and I almost had the tiller pointing in the wrong direction.

However, whatever your level of skill, I'm sure you will find the one particular cake to delight your child, and give you pleasure in the making.

CAROLE HANDSLIP

BASIC TECHNIQUES

Preparation of Cakes

Cakes sometimes cook unevenly. Uneven thickness is usually caused by the cake tin buckling, or the oven temperature being uneven. Excess rising in the middle is caused by the baking temperature being too hot.

With flower pot and basin cakes, cut off the top to achieve an even surface.

With larger tins or Swiss roll tins, it is more successful to invert the cakes; use the base as a surface, filling in any spaces underneath with butter icing. This is necessary for cakes which require a perfectly flat surface.

If cakes are made the day before the party they are much easier to cut to shape. If they are too fresh, the crumbs may stick to the icing and spoil the look of the finished cake.

Cakes can be made well in advance and packed in polythene bags, then frozen to save valuable time on the day. Thaw for about 2 hours before icing.

Preparation of Cake Tins and Basins

Grease the tins with oil, line with greaseproof paper, then grease the paper. Lightly grease basins, then sprinkle with flour. Shake out excess flour.

To Test When a Cake is Done

Press the cake lightly in the centre and it should spring back if it is done. The cake will also begin to shrink slightly from the sides of the tin. Carefully loosen around the sides with a palette knife, leave for 2 minutes, then turn out on to a wire rack to cool completely.

Follow the Novelty Cake Chart for baking time and temperature. Sometimes when there are two sizes of cakes, one will need to be cooked on the lower shelf, where the cooking temperature is slightly less. This is indicated in the chart.

The times should be taken as a guide only, as ovens vary in temperature.

Cake Boards

Cake boards are available in many shapes and sizes – round, square, oblong and heart shaped. If you cannot obtain one to fit your cake, use a tray or piece of hardboard covered with foil. Alternatively, use decorative paper with a waxed surface to cover.

Piping

Royal icing has been used for all decorative purposes such as edges, lines and writing. It is easiest to use a greaseproof piping bag with a No 2 writing nozzle.

Cover the bowl of icing with cling film or a damp cloth to prevent it from drying and forming a crust on top. Any lumps in the icing will cause a blockage in the nozzle and the icing will not flow smoothly, making it extremely difficult to pipe.

To Make a Greaseproof Piping Bag

A greaseproof piping bag is the simplest to use for royal icing. Make several at a time in case the paper splits with the pressure of the icing.

Fold a 25 cm (10 inch) square of greaseproof paper in half to form a triangle.

Hold the apex of the triangle in your left hand, with the point of the apex towards you. Take the right hand point in your right hand, curl the point of paper over until this point and the point of the apex meet, hold them together with the right hand.

With the left hand and the left point of paper, wrap the paper over the top and halfway under the cone, so this point meets the other two points exactly.

Fold the points over twice and crease to secure.

To Fill a Piping Bag

Snip a tiny hole in the point of the bag, insert the nozzle and spoon in some icing until half filled.

Fold the top over, about 1 cm (½ inch). Fold the sides toward the centre, then fold the top over again.

Press the icing from the top to force it out of the nozzle.

To Hold a Piping Bag
Hold the bag near the top, with the folded end between your thumb and fingers.

Squeeze the bag with a gentle, even pressure against the palm of your hand, then guide the nozzle with your free hand. Practice a little before icing the cake.

To Pipe Straight Lines
Squeeze out enough icing to touch the surface then, squeezing the bag gently, lift the nozzle a little above the surface and pull it gently towards you. The icing should flow in a sagging line, which can be manoeuvred to keep straight. To finish, simply touch the surface with the nozzle and stop squeezing.

Writing
Capital letters are probably easiest. Draw the words on greaseproof paper, then carefully lay the paper in position on the iced cake. Mark out the letters by pricking through the paper with a pin. Pipe on top of the pin marks.

Stars
Use a star nozzle and hold the bag upright, just above the surface of the cake. Squeeze the bag gently and make a quick down and up movement to make a squat star.

Moulding Icing

Although I have included a recipe, ready made moulding icing is available in supermarkets, and gives excellent results.

To Ice a Cake
First brush the cake with apricot glaze so that the icing will adhere.

Roll out the icing on a surface dredged with sifted icing sugar to a shape 10 cm (4 inches) larger than the top of the cake.

Support the icing on a sugared rolling pin and place over the cake. Press the icing gently on to the cake and mould, using icing sugar or cornflour on your hands so that the icing does not stick. Rub with a circular movement to give an even covering, then cut off the excess icing.

It is easier to mould joins on a flat surface with a palette knife.

Use egg white as an adhesive when attaching one piece of moulding icing to another.

Roll out trimmings into a ball, knead lightly and re-roll.

To Colour Moulding Icing
Add a few drops of food colouring to the icing, then knead thoroughly until evenly coloured. Use rubber gloves to prevent staining your hands.

Wrap the icing in a polythene bag immediately, as it dries very quickly. If this happens, add a little egg white or water and knead thoroughly.

To Make Decorations
Roll out thinly, cut to shape and leave to dry. For a lily leaf, lift the edges and mould evenly. For a curved leaf, lay over a pencil and leave until dry. Mark veins with the back of a small knife and paint with food colourings. Thin icing will dry within a few hours, thicker icing may need to be left overnight, such as the whale's tail or snooker cues.

This icing has been used to make scarves, towels, the dog's collar, the duck's bill and feet, goblins, canoes, palm trees and similar items.

To Mould Vegetables
Cabbage: Colour some moulding icing or marzipan green, shape a small ball, the size of a pea, for the heart. Shape five or six leaves in the palm of your hand, using icing

sugar to prevent it sticking. Arrange the leaves around the heart, overlapping, and press gently at the base to adhere.
Cauliflower: Make the centre from cream coloured moulding icing, then prick with a fork. Finish as for the cabbage.
Carrot: Use orange moulding icing and shape into small cones. Cut stalks from angelica, then press into the carrot tops.

Note: Moulded decorations can be made up to four weeks in advance and stored in an airtight tin.

To Use Left-over Moulding Icing and Marzipan

Peppermint Creams
Use any left-over moulding icing to make peppermint creams. Knead in a few drops of peppermint flavouring and roll out to a thickness of about 1 cm (½ inch). Cut out with a 2.5 cm (1 inch) plain cutter and leave to dry for 24 hours.

Marzipan Sweets
Use any left-over marzipan to make sweets. Cut out into rounds as for peppermint creams, then dip in melted chocolate. To make marzipan dates, roll the marzipan into short lengths, stuff into a stoned date and roll in caster sugar.

Templates

Some of the recipes require templates, such as swimming pool, tennis racket, ridge tent, disco cake, dinosaur, guitar, grand piano and Concorde.

To make a template, draw the required shape, using the photograph as a guide, on greaseproof paper and cut out. Lay the template on the cake and cut around it, using a sharp, serrated knife held vertically.

Bought Sweets and Decorations

There are so many types of sweets and decorations available that I have made good use of them whenever possible. They add colour and a great deal of excitement!

Liquorice This is used extensively throughout. Sometimes you can buy wide liquorice strips; alternatively, unwind liquorice catherine wheels. These are ideal for eyebrows, bumpers, railway tracks etc. Use pinking shears for a serrated edge, such as owl's eyebrows. Liquorice laces are available in black and red. They are useful for hair, guy ropes, railings etc. To join liquorice laces, heat two ends over a gas flame and press firmly together.
Chocolate Flakes Useful for logs, tree bark or crumbled up for earth.
Matchmakers These are very versatile. Good for logs, legs, ladders, bean poles, fences and supports of all kinds. Stick them together with cooled, melted chocolate. They are also good for use as edible skewers to join cakes together: the Teddy Bear and Dino Dinosaur each have one inserted through the centre of the head and body.
Rolos These make excellent barrels or stools.
Chocolate Thin Mint Crisps Excellent for pavements, paving slabs, roofs, rocket fins and dinosaur spines.
Chocolate Beans These must be the most versatile sweets. They have been used extensively for eyes – just use food colouring to paint in the pupil. Also excellent for headlights, wheel hubs, windows and to add colour on any cake.
Liquorice Allsorts Invaluable for decorating party cakes. Use them for eyes, chimneys, sliced for windows or sills, and white lines on roads.
Other useful sweets are marshmallows, mints, liquorice comfits, candy sticks, silver balls, dolly mixtures, chocolate buttons, lollypops, Polos and hundreds and thousands.

Note: I never use wooden skewers, or any other inedible object, as there is always the danger, especially with small children, that they might cause injury.

To Use Chocolate

Chocolate cake covering is available in plain dark, milk and white. It is cheaper and much easier to use than real chocolate, though the flavour is not so good.

To Melt Chocolate

Break chocolate into pieces and place in a heatproof bowl that fits snugly over a pan of hot water. Bring the water to the boil, turn off the heat, then leave until the chocolate has melted. Heat again if necessary. Do not allow any water to get into the chocolate.

To Coat Cakes

Melt a larger quantity than you think you may need, as coating will be much easier if you can almost submerge the cake. Hold the cake over the bowl to drain off as much chocolate as possible, then leave the coated cake on greaseproof paper to dry.

When set, trim off the excess chocolate at the base and carefully lift off.

To Attach Sweets

Allow melted chocolate to cool, dab a little chocolate on the sweet and hold in position until set.

To Make Blue Jelly

The resulting colour is better if you use a green jelly and colour it blue.

Make the jelly with a little less liquid than usually required, so that it sets more solidly and gives a firmer result when chopped.

Chop the jelly with a sharp knife on dampened greaseproof paper until quite fine.

You can also use 25 g (1 oz) powdered gelatine with 600 ml (1 pint) water, 50 g (2 oz) sugar and blue food colouring for a truer blue colour. I usually make both types of jelly, then mix the two chopped jellies together to give a two-tone sea.

To Use Desiccated Coconut

Desiccated coconut can easily be coloured and is invaluable used as grass, gravel, earth and fur.

To Colour Desiccated Coconut

Put a few drops of water into a bowl and add a few drops of food colouring. Add 225 g (8 oz) desiccated coconut and stir until it is an even colour.

To Coat with Desiccated Coconut or Chocolate Vermicelli

Put the coconut or vermicelli on a piece of greaseproof paper. Place the item to be coated on top, lift the sides of the greaseproof paper and shake until covered.

Alternatively, put the coconut or vermicelli into a polythene bag. Drop in the item to be coated, hold the top together and shake gently until covered.

To Use Wafers

Wafers are extremely useful for windows and doors, fences, running boards etc.

They can also be used to make more sturdy structures such as aeroplane wings, by sandwiching two or three layers together with melted chocolate. Cut wafers very carefully with a serrated-edged knife to obtain a clean edge. Attach them to cakes with melted chocolate or icing.

To Coat the Sides of a Cake

Apply a layer of butter icing to the sides of a cake with a palette knife.

Put the coating, such as chocolate flakes, vermicelli or hundreds and thousands, on a sheet of greaseproof paper. Put the cake on a board and use your hand to support it on the greaseproof paper beside the coating. Use a palette knife to press the decoration evenly on to the sides.

If coating a round cake, hold the cake between the palms of your hands and roll it lightly in the coating until evenly covered. Do this before icing the top.

BASIC RECIPES

Glacé Icing

225 g (8 oz) icing sugar, sifted

flavouring or few drops of food colouring (optional)

Sift the icing sugar into a bowl and gradually add 15–30 ml (1–2 tbsp) warm water. The icing should be thick enough to coat the back of a spoon thickly.

Add the flavouring or colouring and use immediately.

Makes a 225 g (8 oz) quantity

Variations

Coffee: Replace 15 ml (1 tbsp) warm water with 15 ml (1 tbsp) coffee essence.
Orange or Lemon: Replace 15 ml (1 tbsp) warm water with 15 ml (1 tbsp) orange or lemon juice. Add the grated rind of 1 orange or lemon and a few drops of lemon or orange food colouring.
Chocolate: Sift 45 ml (3 tbsp) cocoa powder with the icing sugar.

Royal Icing

1 egg white

225 g (8 oz) icing sugar, sifted

few drops of lemon juice

few drops of food colouring (optional)

Beat the egg white with a fork. Gradually beat in half the icing sugar with a wooden spoon until smooth. Beat in the remaining icing sugar with the lemon juice and colouring, if required.

Cover the bowl with a damp cloth or cling film to prevent the icing drying out. For piping rosettes, it should be fairly firm. For piping writing, the icing should be a little thinner.

Makes a 225 g (8 oz) quantity

Basic Butter Icing

100 g (4 oz) butter

225 (8 oz) icing sugar, sifted

15–30 ml (1–2 tbsp) milk

flavouring or few drops of food colouring (optional)

Beat the butter with half the icing sugar in a bowl until smooth. Add the remaining icing sugar with the milk and any flavouring or colouring. Beat until creamy.

Makes a 225 g (8 oz) quantity

Flavourings

Lemon or Orange: Add the grated rind of 1 lemon or orange to the butter. Replace the milk with lemon or orange juice. Add a few drops of lemon or orange food colouring.
Chocolate: Blend 30 ml (2 tbsp) cocoa powder with 30 ml (2 tbsp) boiling water. Cool, then add to the mixture with a little milk if necessary.
Coffee: Replace 15 ml (1 tbsp) milk with 15 ml (1 tbsp) coffee essence.

Note: Ready made icing is available in tubes in pink, blue, white and chocolate, with fitted piping nozzels if required.

White Soft Icing

100 g (4 oz) white vegetable fat

350 g (12 oz) icing sugar, sifted

3 drops of peppermint flavouring (optional)

Beat the fat with half the icing sugar in a bowl until smooth. Add the remaining icing sugar with 45 ml (3 tbsp) water and the flavouring. Beat until blended.

Makes a 350 g (12 oz) quantity

Moulding Icing

1 egg white

30 ml (1 rounded tbsp) liquid glucose

about 350 g (12 oz) icing sugar, sifted

few drops of food colouring (optional)

Mix the egg white and glucose together in a bowl. Gradually add enough icing sugar to form a stiff paste. Turn on to a surface sprinkled with cornflour and knead until smooth.

Wrap in cling film and keep in a polythene bag to prevent it from drying.

The icing will keep in the refrigerator for up to six weeks. If the icing does become dry, dip it in hot water, wrap and return to the bag for 1 hour, then knead again, adding colouring if using.

Makes a 350 g (12 oz) quantity

Marzipan

350 g (12 oz) ground almonds

175 g (6 oz) icing sugar

175 g (6 oz) caster sugar

1 egg, size 1, beaten

4 drops of almond essence

10 ml (2 tsp) lemon juice

Put the ground almonds and sugars together in a bowl and make a well in the centre. Stir in the egg, almond essence and lemon juice, then mix to a smooth pliable paste. Store in a polythene bag until needed.

Makes about 700 g (1½ lb)

Note: Use this instead of bought marzipan, if preferred.

Chocolate Truffles

Inevitably there will be left-over cake from many of the designs. Make into crumbs and freeze so that you can make these truffles when you have more time. Or serve them for the party tea. These are also useful to form into heads, eg caterpillar.

300 g (10 oz) cake crumbs

50 g (2 oz) caster sugar

30 ml (2 tbsp) cocoa powder, sifted

45 ml (3 tbsp) apricot jam

15 ml (1 tbsp) rum or sherry

1 packet chocolate vermicelli

Put the cake crumbs, sugar, cocoa, jam and rum together in a bowl. Mix to a stiff paste. Form the mixture into balls the size of a walnut. Roll in the chocolate vermicelli until coated. Serve in paper cases.

Variation

Almond Truffles: Omit the cocoa powder and 25 g (1 oz) of the sugar. Replace the rum or sherry with Amaretto liqueur, or almond essence and a little milk. Form into balls and roll in 50 g (2 oz) chopped browned almonds or desiccated coconut.

Apricot Glaze

225 g (8 oz) apricot jam

squeeze of lemon juice

Place the apricot jam and 45 ml (3 tbsp) water into a small pan. Heat until melted. Add the lemon juice, then sieve and return to the pan.

Heat before using. The glaze can be stored in the refrigerator for several months; reheat gently to use.

Madeira Cake

	plain flour	baking powder	butter or margarine	caster sugar	grated lemon rind	eggs	milk
3-egg	225 g (8 oz)	5 ml (1 tsp)	175 g (6 oz)	175 g (6oz)	½	3	30 ml (2 tbsp)
4-egg	300 g (10 oz)	5 ml (1 tsp)	225 g (8 oz)	225 g (8 oz)	½	4	45 ml (3 tbsp)
5-egg	350 g (12 oz)	7.5 ml (1½ tsp)	300 g (10 oz)	300 g (10 oz)	1	5	45 ml (3 tbsp)
6-egg	450 g (1 lb)	10 ml (2 tsp)	350 g (12 oz)	350 g (12 oz)	1	6	60 ml (4 tbsp)

Line and grease the required tin as instructed in the recipe.

Sift the flour and baking powder together and set aside. Cream the butter and sugar together in a bowl with the lemon rind until light and fluffy. Beat in the eggs, one at a time, adding 15 ml (1 tbsp) of flour for each egg after the first 2 eggs. Carefully fold in the remaining flour, then add the milk.

Place the mixture into the prepared tin. Bake at the temperature and time suggested in the Novelty Cake Chart (see pages 16–19). Leave the cake in the tin for 5 minutes, then turn on to a wire rack to cool.

Specialist Shops

There are many specialist cake shops throughout the country, some of which will send items through the post. Here you will find edible wafers in different colours, iced animals, such as ladybirds, frogs, sheep etc, and piping gel. However, most of the decorations I have used have come from supermarkets.

Bought Cakes

I have used bought cakes where possible to save time. Chocolate coated Swiss rolls, both large and small, are very useful. The larger luxury Swiss rolls are more successful than the cheaper thin variety.

Oblong Madeira cakes, both vanilla and chocolate, are firm and make a good base for many of the cakes. Choose ones with as flat a top as possible.

Victoria Sandwich Cake

	butter or margarine	caster sugar	eggs	self raising flour	hot water
2-egg	125 g (4 oz)	125 g (4 oz)	2	125 g (4 oz)	15 ml (1 tbsp)
3-egg	175 g (6 oz)	175 g (6 oz)	3	175 g (6 oz)	15 ml (1 tbsp)
4-egg	225 g (8 oz)	225 g (8 oz)	4	225 g (8 oz)	30 ml (2 tbsp)
5-egg	300 g (10 oz)	300 g (10 oz)	5	300 g (10 oz)	45 ml (3 tbsp)
6-egg	350 g (12 oz)	350 g (12 oz)	6	350 g (12 oz)	45 ml (3 tbsp)
9-egg	500 g (1 lb 2oz)	500 g (1 lb 2 oz)	9	500 g (1 lb 2 oz)	75 ml (5 tbsp)

Line and grease the required tin as instructed in the recipe.

Cream the butter and sugar together in a bowl until light and fluffy. Beat in the eggs, one at a time, adding 15 ml (1 tbsp) of flour for each egg after the first one. Fold in the remaining flour with a metal spoon, then add the hot water. Place the mixture into the prepared tin. Bake at the temperature and time suggested in the Novelty Cake Chart (see pages 16–19) until the cake springs back when lightly pressed. Turn on to a wire rack to cool.

Variations

Chocolate: Blend 15 ml (1 tbsp) cocoa powder with 15 ml (1 tbsp) hot water. Cool slightly, then beat in with the butter and sugar.
Coffee: Add 15 ml (1 tbsp) instant coffee powder with the flour.
Orange or Lemon: Add the grated rind of 1 orange or lemon with the butter and sugar. Replace the water with orange or lemon juice.

Note: These variations are for a 2-egg Victoria sandwich. If making a larger cake, adjust the quantities accordingly.

Food Processor Cake

125 g (4 oz) soft margarine
125 g (4 oz) caster sugar
2 eggs
125 g (4 oz) self raising flour, sifted
5 ml (1 tsp) sifted baking powder

Put all the ingredients in a food processor and blend for 1–2 minutes until smooth. Turn into the prepared tin.

Note: This mixture is suitable for use in Swiss roll tins, 18×28 cm (7×11 inch) baking tins or sandwich tins. It is not successful used for deep cakes, such as basins and flowerpots.

NOVELTY CAKE CHART

Cake	*Cake Mixture*	*Tin Size*	*Oven Temperature*	*Time*
Sid Snail	4-egg Madeira	1 litre (2 pt) basin 18 cm (7 in) shallow square tin 1 cup cake	170°C (325°F) mark 3 bottom shelf top shelf	1¾–2 hrs 35–40 mins 20 mins
Dancing Flower	3-egg Madeira	900 ml (1½ pt) flower pot	170°C (325°F) mark 3	1½ hrs
Boxing Ring	3-egg Madeira	18 cm (7 in) deep square tin	170°C (325°F) mark 3	1¼–1½ hrs
Dilly Duck	3-egg Victoria Sandwich	20 cm (8 in) sandwich tin 13 cm (5 in) round tin	180°C (350°F) mark 4 (Put just half the mixture in the 20 cm [8 in] sandwich tin)	35–40 mins 35 mins
Winnie Whale	4-egg Madeira	20×30 cm (8×12 in) Swiss roll tin 600 ml (1 pt) basin	180°C (350°F) mark 4 top shelf bottom shelf	30 mins 1 hr
Thatched Cottage	5-egg Madeira	20 cm (8 in) square tin	170°C (325°F) mark 3	1¾–2 hrs
Valentine Cake	3-egg Madeira	20 cm (8 in) deep heart tin	170°C (325°F) mark 3	1½–1¾ hrs
Wicked Witch	4-egg Victoria Sandwich	18 cm (7 in) shallow square tin 18×28 cm (7×11 in) oblong tin	180°C (350°F) mark 4	25–30 mins 30–35 mins
Porky Pig	4-egg Madeira	900 ml (1½ pt) basin 600 ml (1 pt) basin 1 cup cake	170°C (325°F) mark 3	1½–1¾ hrs 1½ hrs 20 mins

Cake	*Cake Mixture*	*Tin Size*	*Oven Temperature*	*Time*
Percy Penguin	3-egg Madeira	two 450 ml (¾ pt) basins 793 g (1 lb 12 oz) can	180°C (350°F) mark 4 (to obtain a rounded top)	45–50 mins
Freddie Frog/ Ozzie Owl	4-egg Madeira	600 ml (1 pt) basin 900 ml (1½ pt) basin	170°C (325°F) mark 3	1½ hrs 1½–1¾ hrs
Sandcastle	4-egg Madeira	1 litre (2 pt) flower pot 3 dariole moulds	170°C (325°F) mark 3	1½–1¾ hrs 35 mins
Noah's Ark	6-egg Madeira	900 g (2 lb) loaf tin 450 g (1 lb) loaf tin 600 ml (1 pt) basin	170°C (325°F) mark 3	1¼ hrs 1 hr 1½ hrs
Sammy Spider	3-egg Madeira	1 litre (2 pt) basin	180°C (350°F) mark 4	1¼–1½ hrs
Tommy Turtle	5-egg Madeira	4 litre (7 pt) basin 18 cm (7 in) shallow square tin	170°C (325°F) mark 3	1¼–1½ hrs 30–35 mins
Teddy Bear	5-egg Madeira	900 ml (1½ pt) basin 600 ml (1 pt) basin 18 cm (7 in) sandwich tin	170°C (325°F) mark 3	1½–1¾ hrs 1½ hrs 35–40 mins
Buzzy Bumble Bee	3-egg Madeira	900 ml (1½ pt) basin 450 ml (¾ pt) basin	170°C (325°F) mark 3	1½–1¾ hrs 1 hr
Dino Dinosaur	4-egg Victoria Sandwich	two 20 cm (8 in) sandwich tins	170°C (325°F) mark 3	40 mins

Cake	*Cake Mixture*	*Tin Size*	*Oven Temperature*	*Time*
Toadstool and Goblins	4-egg Madeira	2.3 litre (4 pt) basin 793 g (1 lb 12 oz) can	170°C (325°F) mark 3 (half fill can and put rest in the bowl)	1½ hrs 1¼ hrs
Sailing Boat	3-egg Madeira	two 450 g (1 lb) loaf tins	170°C (325°F) mark 3	50–60 mins
Paddock/ Vegetable Patch	4-egg Victoria Sandwich	20 × 30 cm (8 × 12 in) Swiss roll tin, lined 2.5 cm (1 in) up each side	190°C (375°F) mark 5	20–25 mins
Treasure Island	4-egg Victoria Sandwich	20 × 30 cm (8 × 12 in) Swiss roll tin, lined 2.5 cm (1 in) up each side 600 ml (1 pt) basin	190°C (375°F) mark 5 (Put 60 ml [4 tbsp] in basin and rest in the Swiss roll tin)	20–25 mins 20 mins
Athletic Track	5-egg Victoria Sandwich	20 × 30 cm (8 × 12 in) Swiss roll tin 20 cm (8 in) sandwich tin	190°C (375°F) mark 5 lower shelf	20–25 mins 35–40 mins
Guitar	6-egg Victoria Sandwich	two 20 × 30 cm (8 × 12 in) Swiss roll tins	190°C (375°F) mark 5	25–30 mins
Grand Piano	3-egg Victoria Sandwich	20 × 30 cm (8 × 12 in) Swiss roll tin	190°C (375°F) mark 5	25–30 mins
Rosie Rabbit	3-egg Victoria Sandwich	20 cm (8 in) sandwich tin 12.5 cm (5 in) round tin two 8 cm (3¼ in) barquette moulds	180°C (350°F) mark 4	35–40 mins 30–35 mins 20–25 mins
Man on the Moon	5-egg Madeira	4 litre (7 pt) basin	170°C (325°F) mark 3	1½–1¾ hrs

Cake	*Cake Mixture*	*Tin Size*	*Oven Temperature*	*Time*
Mary, Mary, Quite Contrary	3-egg Madeira	1 litre (2 pt) flower pot 1 dariole mould	170°C (325°F) mark 3	1½ hrs 35 mins
Digby Dog	4-egg Madeira	600 ml (1 pt) basin 900 ml (1½ pt) basin 1 dariole mould	170°C (325°F) mark 3	1½ hrs 1½–1¾ hrs 35 mins
Tennis Racket	3-egg Victoria Sandwich	20 × 30 cm (8 × 12 in) Swiss roll tin	190°C (375°F) mark 5	25–30 mins
Cricket Bat	2-egg Victoria Sandwich	20 × 30 cm (8 × 12 in) Swiss roll tin	190°C (375°F) mark 5	20–25 mins
Hovercraft	6-egg Victoria Sandwich	two 18 × 28 cm (7 × 11 in) tins 18 cm (7 in) sandwich tin	180°C (350°F) mark 4	30–35 mins 35–40 mins
Snooker Table	5-egg Victoria Sandwich	20 × 30 cm (8 × 12 in) Swiss roll tin 18 × 28 cm (7 × 11 in) tin	190°C (375°F) mark 5 lower shelf	25–30 mins 30–35 mins
Swimming Pool	6-egg Victoria Sandwich	two 20 × 30 cm (8 × 12 in) Swiss roll tins 1 dariole mould	190°C (375°F) mark 5	25–30 mins 35 mins
Big Red Bus	9-egg Victoria Sandwich	three 18 × 28 cm (7 × 11 in) tins	180°C (350°F) mark 4	30–35 mins
Disco Cake	3-egg Victoria Sandwich	20 × 30 cm (8 × 12 in) Swiss roll tin	190°C (375°F) mark 5	25–35 mins

PORKY PIG

4-egg Madeira cake mixture baked in a 600 ml (1 pint) basin, 900 ml (1½ pint) basin and 1 cup cake
•
50 g (2 oz) butter icing
•
apricot glaze
•
450 g (1 lb) pink moulding icing
•
egg white
•
black food colouring
•
chocolate beans
•
4 marshmallows

1 Lay the large basin cake on its flat surface and remove an angled slice as shown.

2 Stick the cut slice on top of the large basin cake with butter icing. Position the flat surface of the small basin cake on to the cut area. Cut a slice off the cup cake as shown to form the snout.

3 Position the snout on to the head. Brush all the cakes with apricot glaze.

4 Roll out a little pink moulding icing and cut ears to shape. To make the tail, roll out a thin string of icing and wrap around a thin wooden skewer. Leave to set before removing.

5 Roll out three-quarters of the pink moulding icing and cut out a 28 cm (11 inch) round. Lay over the body and mould to shape. Trim off the excess icing. Roll out the remaining icing with the trimmings and cut out a 24 cm (9½ inch) round. Lay over the head and mould to shape. Trim off the excess icing. Roll out all the trimmings and cut out a 12.5 cm (5 inch) round to cover the snout. Mould to shape and trim off the excess icing.

6 Attach the snout to the face using egg white and balance in position until set. Attach the ears and tail with egg white and balance with cocktail sticks until set. Remove the sticks before serving.

7 Using black food colouring, paint a black pupil in the centre of two chocolate beans for eyes and stick in position with butter icing. Stick two chocolate bean nostrils on the snout with butter icing. Cut four marshmallows almost in half with a sharp knife and place in position as trotters.

STEP

1

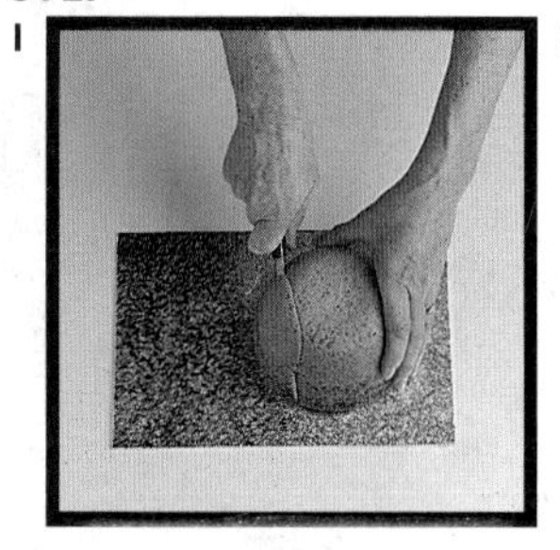

2

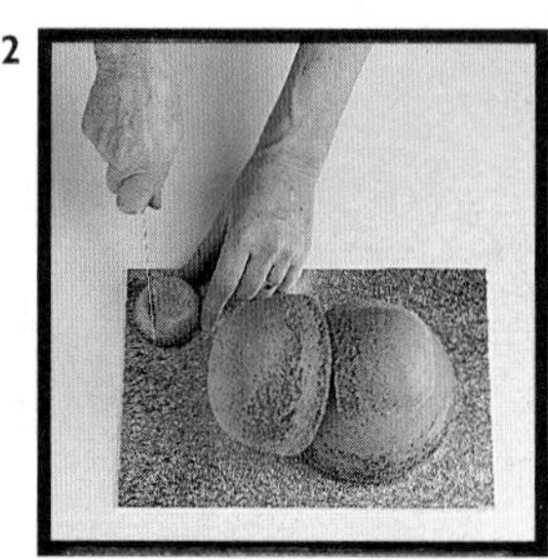

3

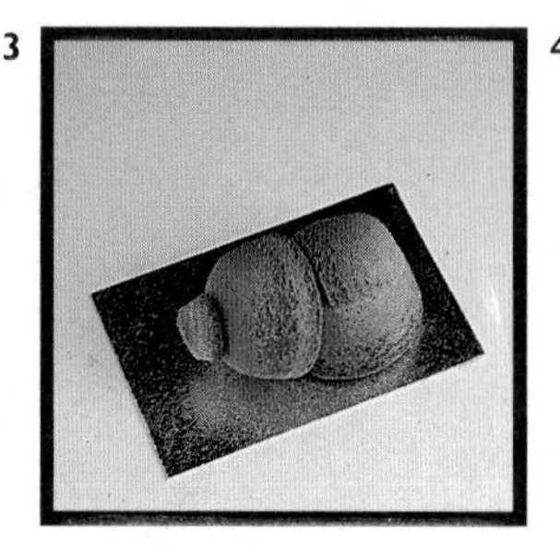

4

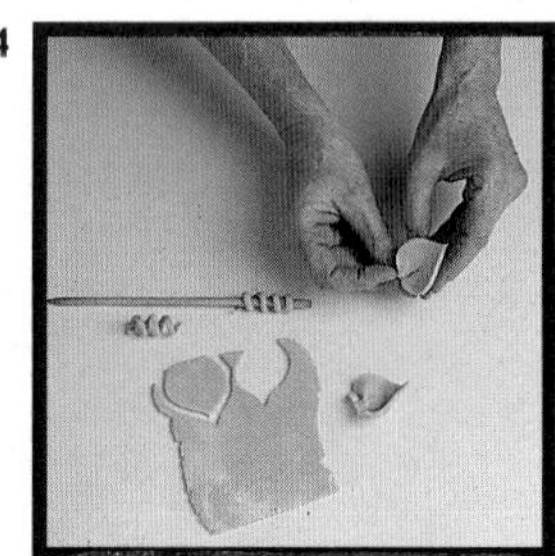

DANCING FLOWER

3-egg Madeira cake mixture baked in a 900 ml (1½ pint) flower pot
•
apricot glaze
•
350 g (12 oz) terracotta marzipan
•
egg white
•
50 g (2 oz) chocolate butter icing
•
chocolate flakes
•
red edible wafers
•
white edible wafers
•
green food colouring
•
striped candy stick
•
15 ml (1 tbsp) royal icing
•
liquorice allsorts

1 Brush the cake with apricot glaze.
2 Roll the terracotta marzipan into a curved shape measuring about 12.5 × 30 cm (5 × 12 inches).
3 Lay the cake on one end of the marzipan and roll up to cover the cake to extend 0.5 cm (¼ inch) at the top. Cut to size and mould the join with a palette knife. Fold excess marzipan under at the base.
4 Brush the top 2 cm (¾ inch) of the flower pot with a little egg white. Roll out a strip of marzipan measuring 2.5 × 43 cm (1 × 17 inches) and wrap around the top of the flower pot, cutting off any excess and moulding the join with a palette knife.
5 Spread butter icing carefully over the top of the cake and sprinkle with chocolate flakes.
6 Cut petals from red edible wafers and leaves from white wafer. Paint the white wafer with green food colouring and leave to dry. Stick the petals on to one end of the candy stick with royal icing to resemble a flower. Stick liquorice eyes and a mouth on to the petals with icing and leave to dry. Stick the leaves on to the stalk and leave to dry, laying flat.
7 Make a hole in the centre of the flower pot with a 0.5 cm (¼ inch) wooden skewer. Press the flower into the flower pot.

STEP

2

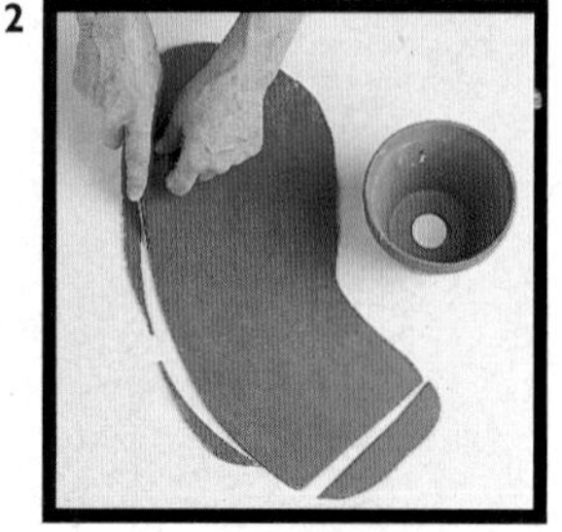

3

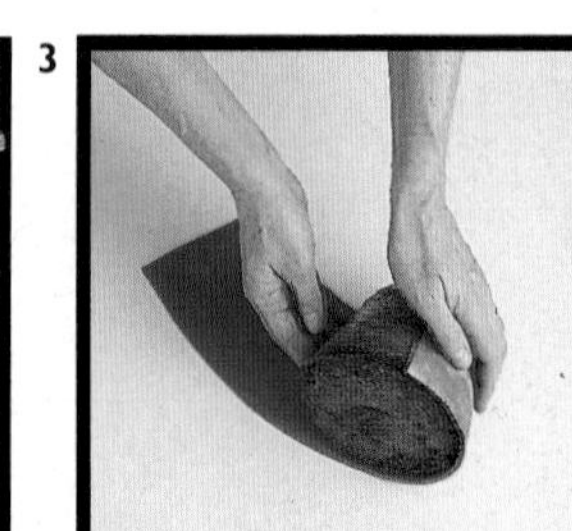

4

6

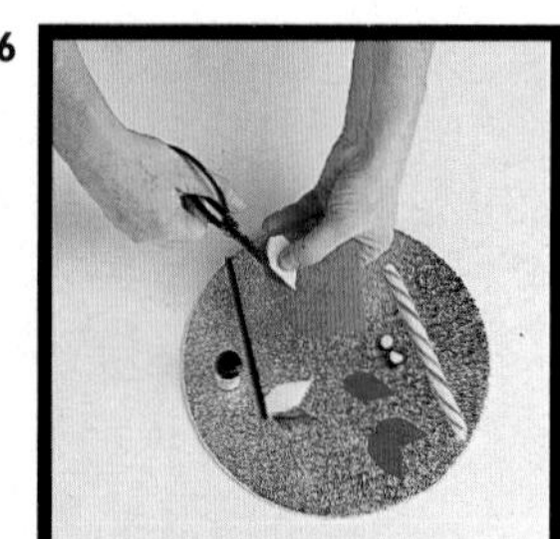

SPACE SHIP

three 23 cm (9 inch) bought sponge cake layers
•
100 g (4 oz) vanilla butter icing
•
1 sponge madeleine
•
apricot glaze
•
450 g (1 lb) white moulding icing
•
mini Swiss rolls
•
white marshmallows
•
chocolate beans
•
liquorice comfits
•
50 g (2 oz) red royal icing
•
red or silver ball
•
2 liquorice allsorts
•
2 lollies

1 Sandwich the sponge layers together with the vanilla butter icing.
2 Cut the curved base off the madeleine and discard. Brush the cake with apricot glaze and cover with white moulding icing for the pod.
3 Cut the mini Swiss rolls in half horizontally, then in half vertically. Attach to the outside edge of the cake with icing. Brush the cake with apricot glaze.
4 Roll out the white moulding icing to a 32 cm (12½ inch) round and lay over the cake.
5 Shape and mould the side of the cake to a pointed edge.
6 Put the pod in position on top of the space ship, attaching with icing.
7 Arrange two circles of marshmallows on a cake board to support the cake. Place the space ship in position on top.
8 Stick chocolate beans around the edge of the space ship with icing. Position liquorice comfits on top and pipe restraining straps on top with red royal icing. Pipe windows on the pod with red icing and stick a red or silver ball on top.
9 Stick a liquorice allsort in position on both sides of the cake with icing and attach a lolly on top with icing.

STEP

2

3

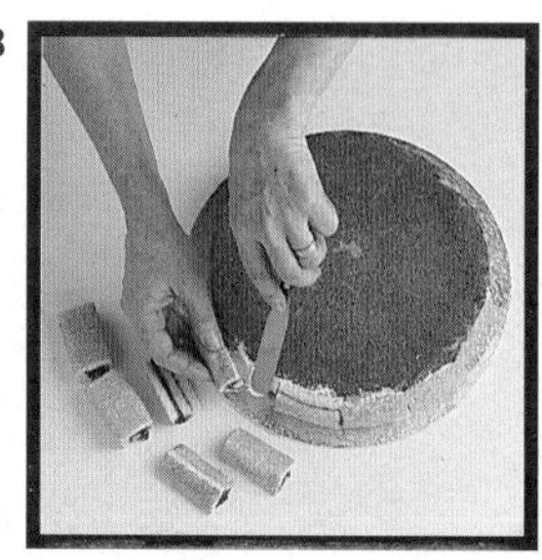

5

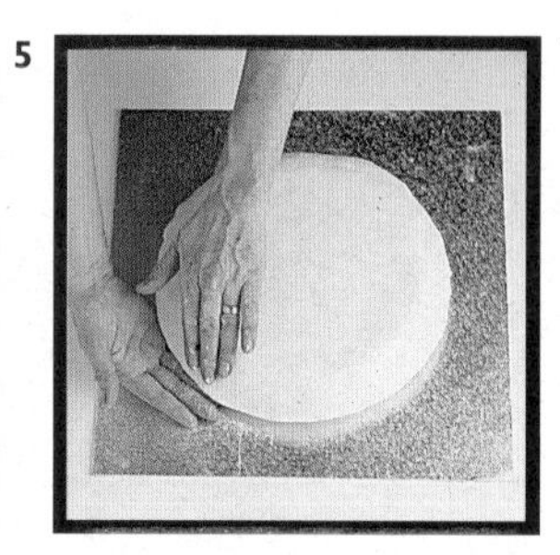

7

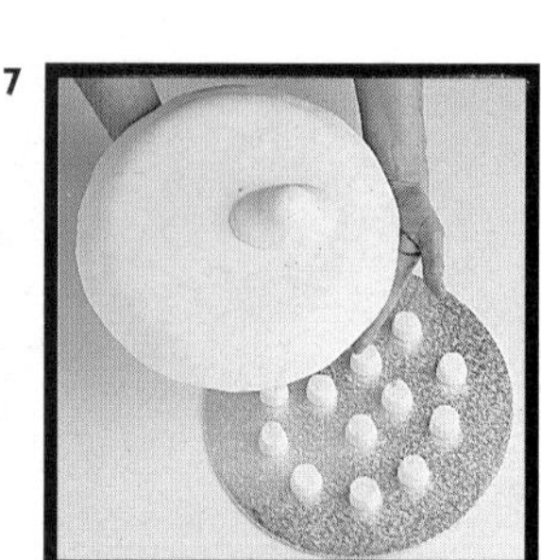

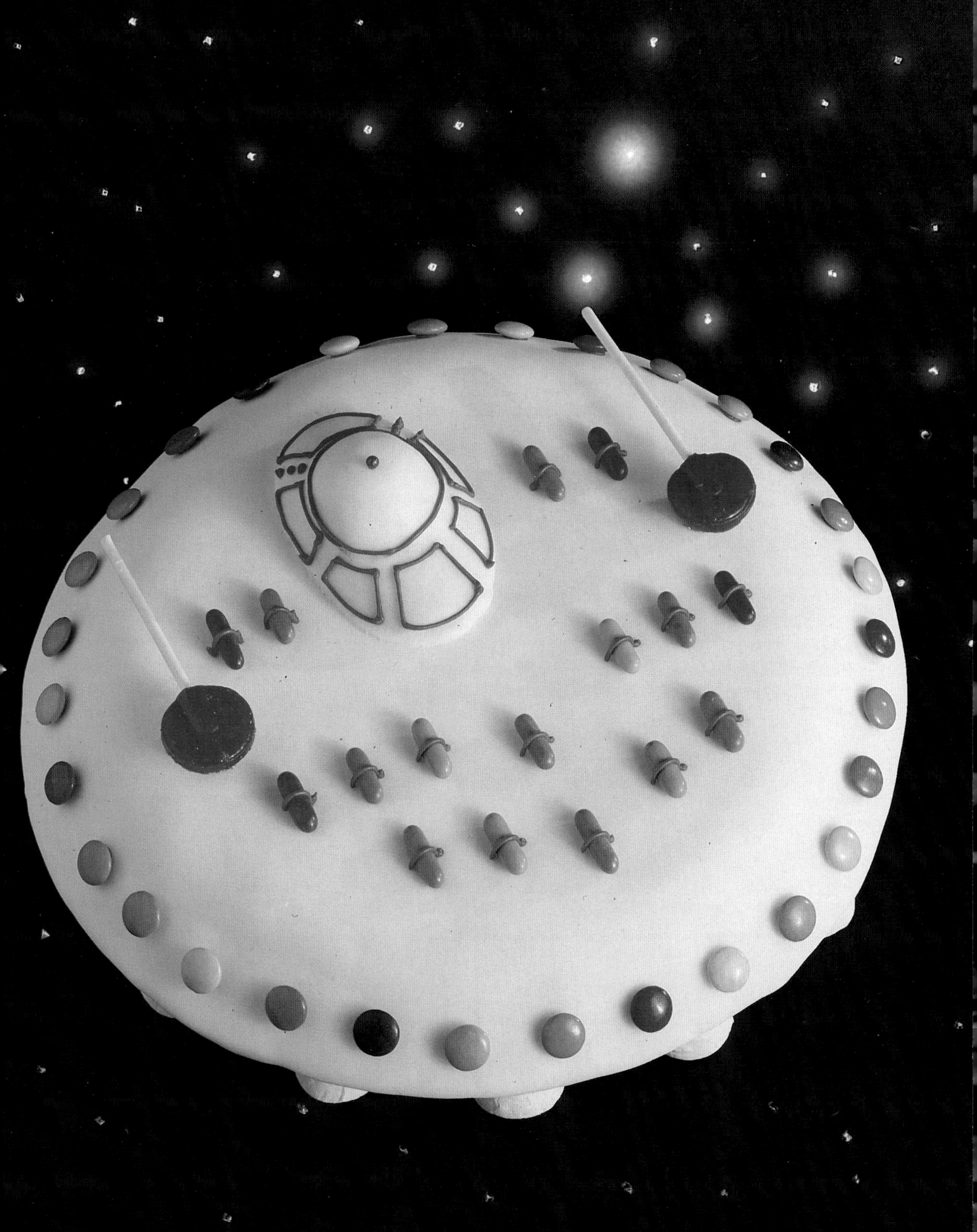

DILLY DUCK

3-egg Victoria sandwich mixture baked in a 20 cm (8 inch) sandwich tin and 13 cm (5 inch) round tin

•

225 g (8 oz) yellow butter icing

•

225 g (8 oz) orange moulding icing

•

50 g (2 oz) orange butter icing

•

2 liquorice allsorts

•

chopped blue jelly

1 Cut the large cake in half lenthways and sandwich together with butter icing to make the body.
2 Cut the head, tail and back from the small cake as shown.
3 Stand the body on a cake board, supporting with a wedge of cake. Trim the front of the head slightly. Stick the head, tail and back in position with icing.
4 Roll out the orange moulding icing and cut out the wings, bill and feet shapes. Leave to dry.
5 Cover the duck with the yellow butter icing and use a palette knife to flick the icing to resemble feathers. Ice the wings and attach to the body. Fleck the wings, head and tail with orange butter icing. Put the feet and bill in position.
6 Put liquorice allsorts in position for the eyes. Surround the duck with chopped blue jelly.

Note: Do not assemble the duck too far in advance or the weight of the moulding icing may cause the wings to drop off.

STEP

1

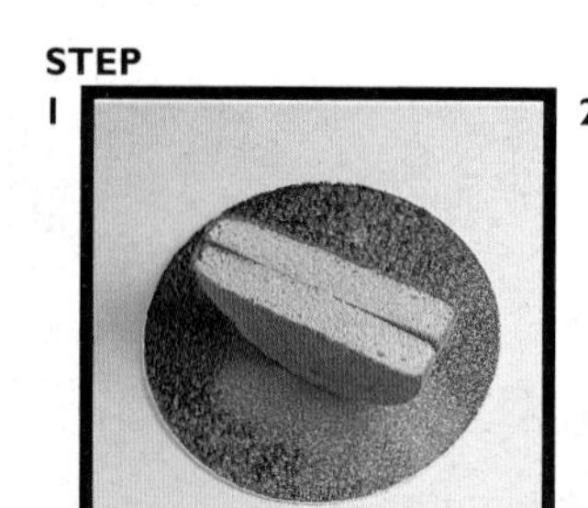

2

3

4

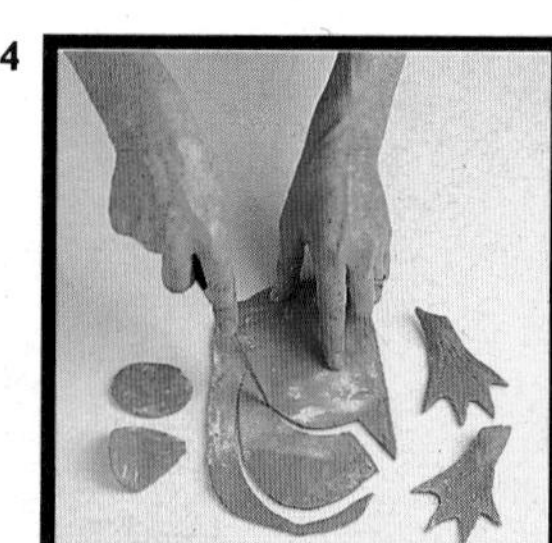

TENNIS RACKET

3-egg Victoria sandwich mixture baked in a 20 × 30 cm (8 × 12 inch) Swiss roll tin
•
apricot glaze
•
225 g (8 oz) green moulding icing
•
225 g (8 oz) coffee moulding icing
•
3 mini chocolate coated Swiss rolls
•
100 g (4 oz) chocolate moulding icing
•
100 g (4 oz) yellow royal icing
•
50 g (2 oz) red royal icing
•
1 large almond truffle (see page 13)
•
yellow desiccated coconut

1 Invert the cake so that the top is level, then cut using a template. Brush with apricot glaze.
2 Roll out the green moulding icing, cut to shape and lay on top of the cake on a cake board.
3 Roll out the coffee moulding icing and cut into 4 cm (1½ inch) wide strips. Lay the strips around the sides of the cake and over the top edge to form the frame of the racket.
4 Insert a piece of coffee moulding icing to complete the racket shape.
5 Brush the mini Swiss rolls with apricot glaze. Cover one of them with coffee moulding icing, place in position and mould the join together.
6 Roll the chocolate moulding icing into strips, 2 cm (¾ inch) wide. Lay diagonally over the two remaining mini Swiss rolls, cutting off the excess icing. Place in position as the handle on the cake board.
7 Using yellow royal icing, pipe in the strings of the racket. Pipe red royal icing on the racket to decorate as shown.
8 For the ball, make a large almond truffle with the leftover cake. Brush with apricot glaze and shake in yellow coconut.

STEP

1

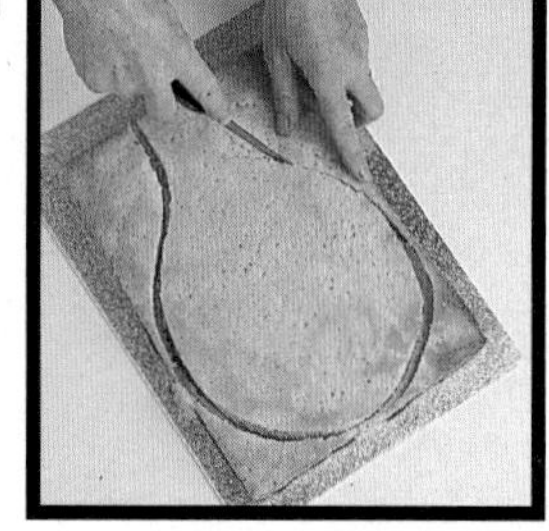

3

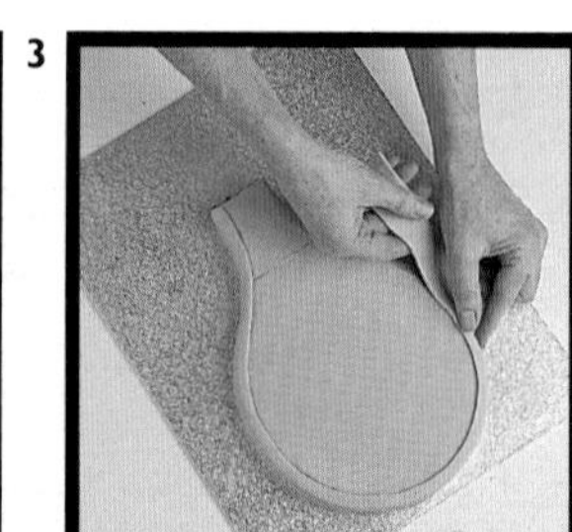

4

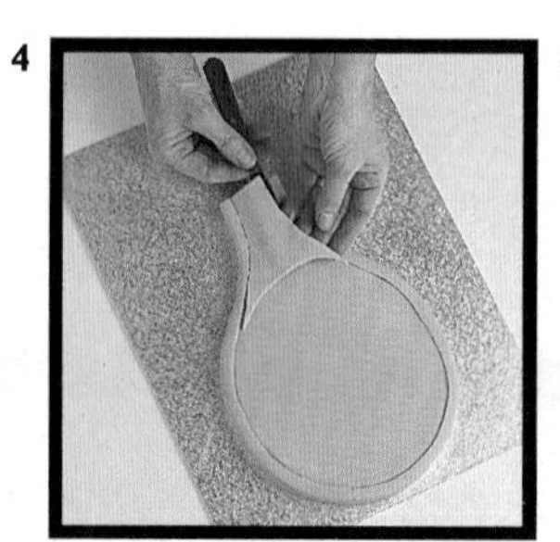

6

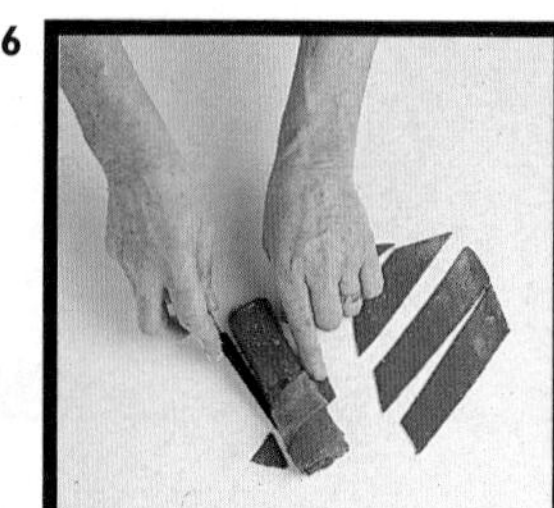

HOVERCRAFT

6-egg Victoria sandwich mixture baked in two 18 × 28 cm (7 × 11 inch) tins, 18 cm (7 inch) sandwich tin

100 g (4 oz) chocolate butter icing

8 mini Swiss rolls

apricot glaze

225 g (8 oz) chocolate moulding icing

225 g (8 oz) red moulding icing

225 g (8 oz) white moulding icing

5 sandwich wafer biscuits

25 g (1 oz) melted white chocolate

wafers

4 candy sticks

50 g (2 oz) red royal icing

50 g (2 oz) white royal icing

chocolate beans

1 Cut the round cake in half vertically and sandwich together with chocolate butter icing. Sandwich the long cakes together with butter icing, inverting the top cake to give a flat surface and cut the sides vertically to straighten. Stick to the round cake with butter icing and put on a cake board. Round off the square ends of the top of the cake only.

2 Trim the ends off the mini Swiss rolls. Cut in half lengthways and place all around the base of the cake, cutting them in half to fit neatly around the circular cake and sticking with butter icing.

3 Brush the cakes all over with apricot glaze. Roll out the chocolate moulding icing into two strips about 7.5 cm (3 inches) wide and lay over the mini rolls to form the skirt.

4 Roll out the red moulding icing and cut into two strips about 2.5 cm (1 inch) wide and attach to the side of the hovercraft. Roll out the white moulding icing, cut to size and lay over the top of the cake.

5 Stick three wafer biscuits together with melted chocolate, cut to shape to form the cabin, glaze and cover with red moulding icing. Cut the remaining wafer biscuits in half horizontally, then cut to shape as shown, making four propellor shafts and two larger tail fins. Brush with apricot glaze, cover the two larger ones with white moulding icing and remainder with red moulding icing.

6 Cut the wafers into thin strips and stick on to a candy stick with melted white chocolate. Attach to a red propellor shaft. Repeat with the three others.

7 Decorate with red and white royal icing and chocolate beans, as liked. Fix the cabin, tail fins and propellor shafts in position with icing.

STEP

1

2

5

6

DIGBY DOG

4-egg Madeira cake mixture baked in a 600 ml (1 pint) basin, 900 ml (1½ pint) basin and 1 dariole mould
•
225 g (8 oz) vanilla butter icing
•
2 sponge fingers
•
100 g (4 oz) chocolate butter icing
•
2 chocolate beans
•
1 liquorice sweet
•
25 g (1 oz) red moulding icing
•
gold balls
•
white marzipan (optional)

1 Cut the tops from both basin cakes, then place, rounded sides up, on a board.
2 For the body of the dog, shape the slice from the smaller cake and stick on top of the larger cake with icing.
3 Using the remaining slice of cake, cut the hind legs and tail as shown. Cut a diagonal slice from the sponge fingers for the front paws.
4 Assemble the dog, using the small basin cake for the head. Cut a slice from the wide end of the dariole mould and cut in half for the ears. Cut a small piece to form the neck and nose.
5 Coat the basin cakes and all shaped pieces with vanilla butter icing, attaching legs, ears, nose and tail in position.
6 Use chocolate butter icing to give a mottled effect to the dog's coat, using a fork. Add chocolate beans for the eyes and a liquorice sweet for the nose.
7 Make a collar from the red moulding icing and lay around the dog's neck. Press on gold balls for the studs. Make a bone from the white marzipan, if liked.

STEP 1

2

3

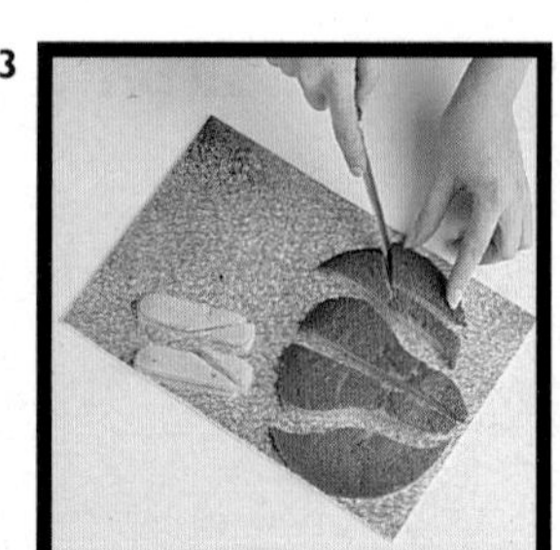

4

PERCY PENGUIN

3-egg Madeira cake mixture baked in a 793 g (1 lb 12 oz) can and two 450 ml (¾ pint) basins

•

100 g (4 oz) soft white icing

•

225 g (8 oz) black butter icing

•

liquorice comfits

•

2 chocolate beans

•

50 g (2 oz) red moulding icing

1 Cut the rounded top from one of the basin cakes, cut in half and reserve for the wings.

2 Cut off the top of the can cake to make it level. Stick the basin cake on top of the can cake and trim to fit exactly.

3 Round off the edges of the second basin cake to form the head. Cut a slice from the side and attach to the body with icing. Attach the wings to each side of the body.

4 Coat the front of the body with soft white icing. Coat the head, wings and the rest of the body with black butter icing.

5 Cut a yellow liquorice comfit in half lengthways and insert for the beak. Use orange liquorice comfits for the feet. Position chocolate beans for the eyes.

6 Roll out the red moulding icing into a strip and make into a scarf as shown, then lay around the neck of the penguin.

STEP

1

2

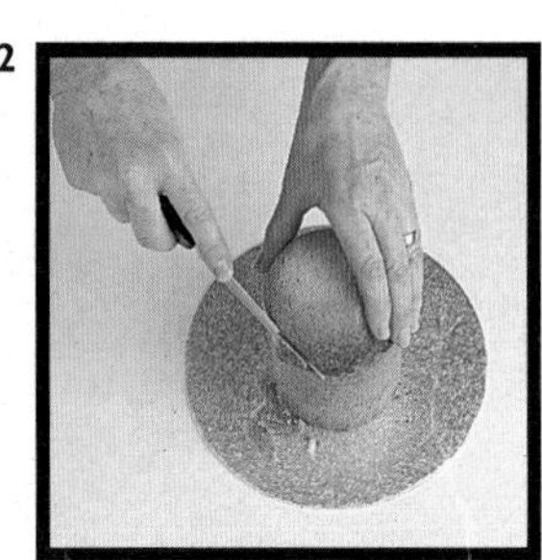

3

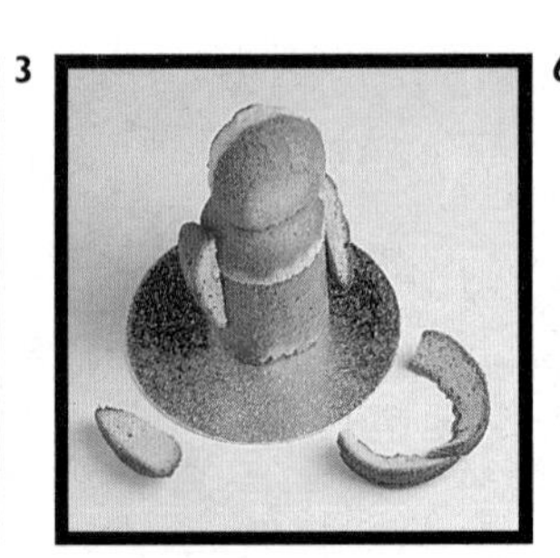

6

GRAND PIANO

3-egg Victoria sandwich mixture baked in a 20 × 30 cm (8 × 12 inch) Swiss roll tin
•
225 g (8 oz) melted chocolate
•
100 g (4 oz) chocolate butter icing
•
apricot glaze
•
225 g (8 oz) marzipan
•
175 g (6 oz) chocolate moulding icing
•
225 g (8 oz) white marzipan
•
black royal icing
•
50 g (2 oz) white royal icing
•
50 g (2 oz) red royal icing
•
2 Matchmakers
•
3 ice cream cones
•
3 chocolate buttons

1 Cut a template from a piece of greaseproof paper, measuring 18 × 28 cm (7 × 11 inches), into the shape of the piano as shown. Cut the cake into two pieces, using the template.

2 Cut a 2 cm (¾ inch) slice from the end of one piece and discard.

3 Cut a thin slice from the top of the shorter piece for the lid. Lay the slice on greaseproof paper and coat with melted chocolate. Leave to set, then turn over and coat the other side. Leave to set.

4 Spread the surface of the longer cake with chocolate butter icing and lay the shorter piece of cake on top. Trim the narrow end to shape and brush the cake with apricot glaze. Cut a board slightly smaller than the template and put the cake on it.

5 Roll out the marzipan and cut to fit the top of the piano, using the template.

6 Roll out the chocolate moulding icing into two long strips and use to coat the sides of the cake.

7 Roll out the white marzipan and cut to fit the ledge, forming the keyboard. Use a small knife to mark the keys in the marzipan. Pipe black royal icing on the keyboard to form the sharps and flats.

8 Roll out the remaining white marzipan and cut to shape for a thin border around the edge. Pipe the strings with white royal icing, finishing each end with a dot of red royal icing. Stick a half Matchmaker on each side of the piano front.

9 To make the legs, cut 5 cm (2 inches) from the flared top of each cone and cut off the tip of each one. Dip in melted chocolate, stand the pointed end on a chocolate button and leave to set.

10 Balance the piano on the legs. Support the lid in position with a Matchmaker standing on a chocolate button.

Note: Make the template as accurate as possible as the cut is critical. Support the lid in position just before the party.

STEP

1
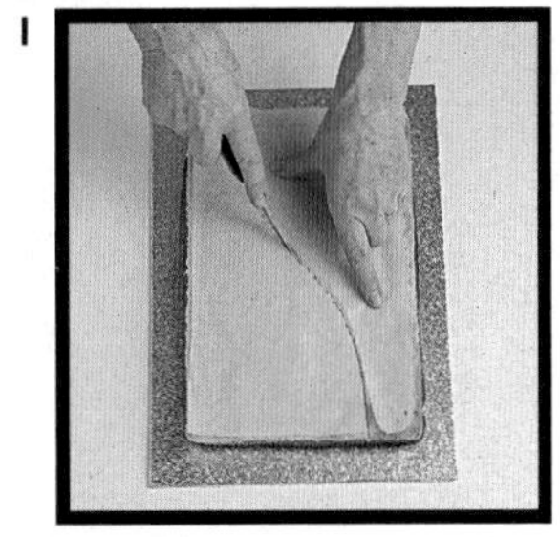

2

3

4

BACH

FAIRY CASTLE

3 bought oblong Madeira cakes
•
225 g (8 oz) pink butter icing
•
3 Swiss rolls
•
5 ice cream cones
•
100 g (4 oz) soft white icing
•
hundreds and thousands
•
coconut ice sweets
•
wafers
•
sugar flowers
•
50 g (2 oz) green royal icing
•
50 g (2 oz) green butter icing
•
50 g (2 oz) blue butter icing

1 Stick the three Madeira cakes together in the upright position with pink butter icing. Cut off a 2.5 cm (1 inch) triangular section from each corner.

2 Cut a third from each Swiss roll. Stand the long pieces upright in each corner, sticking with icing. Stick two of the remaining pieces together to make the fourth central turret.

3 Stick the removed triangular corners together with icing to make a square. Cover with icing and place on top of the cake in the centre. Put the remaining piece of Swiss roll on top of the square for the central turret.

4 Cover the cake and Swiss rolls with pink butter icing and smooth evenly with a palette knife.

5 Cover the five cones with soft white icing. Mark into peaks with a palette knife, then sprinkle lightly with hundreds and thousands. Attach to the turrets with icing.

6 Cut the coconut ice into slices and stick around the top of the cake to form battlements.

7 Shape the wafers to make doors and windows, then press into position. Decorate the walls with sugar flowers and pipe on stalks and leaves with green royal icing.

8 Using a rosette nozzle, pipe soft white icing around the base of each cone and around the door. Pipe pink icing around the windows and elsewhere as liked.

9 Coat a wafer with icing and dip into hundreds and thousands to cover completely. Spread green and blue icing on the cake board to represent grass and the moat. Lay the coated wafer over the moat as a drawbridge.

Note: There is no need to pipe the castle if you want to make the cake more simple.

STEP

1

2

3

5
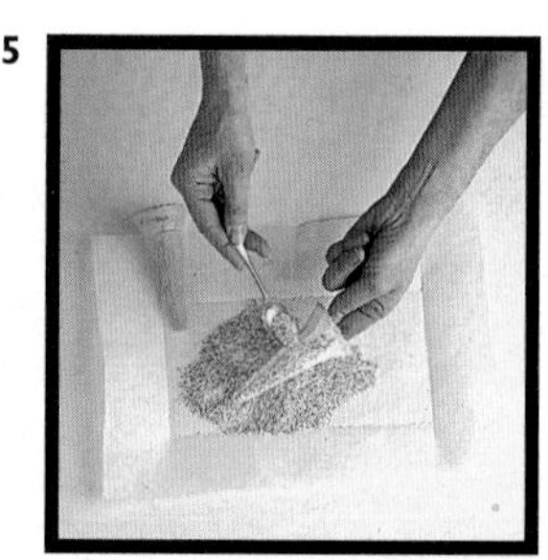

AEROPLANE

wafers
•
100 g (4 oz) melted white chocolate
•
1 chocolate coated Swiss roll
•
1 mini chocolate coated Swiss roll
•
1 chocolate coated teacake
•
50 g (2 oz) melted chocolate
•
1 ice cream cone
•
50 g (2 oz) red royal icing
•
Matchmakers
•
liquorice allsorts
•
chocolate decorations

1 Make the wings by laying three wafers end to end on greaseproof paper as shown. Spread with melted white chocolate, then lay three more wafers on top, cutting the third wafer in half to fill in at each end. Repeat for the second wing, cover with a wooden board and leave to dry.

2 Lay the large Swiss roll on the small one, inserting one wing as shown. Cut the top off the teacake and stick the cut surface to the Swiss roll with melted chocolate. Stick the second wing on top with melted chocolate.

3 Shape three wafers as shown for the tail plane. Stick together with melted white chocolate, inserting the upright between the two wafers. Press firmly together.

4 Cut the cone at the top of the flared section and cut the top 2.5 cm (1 inch) from the tip of the cone. Dip each end of the flared cone into melted chocolate. Stick to the cake with melted chocolate. Insert the pointed piece of cone, sticking with chocolate. Cut the propellor to shape from a wafer and stick on to the nose.

5 Pipe red royal icing around the nose cone, wing edges and tail plane. Position Matchmakers between the wings, sticking with melted chocolate.

6 Cut the number and roundel from liquorice allsorts, then stick on to the fuselage with melted chocolate. Attach chocolate decorations to the wings with melted chocolate.

STEP

1

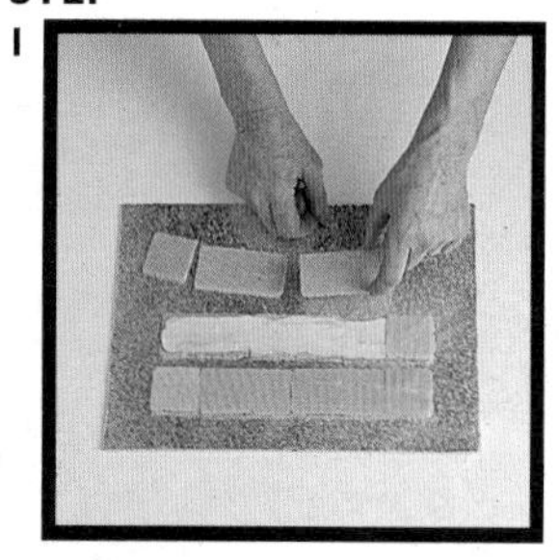

2

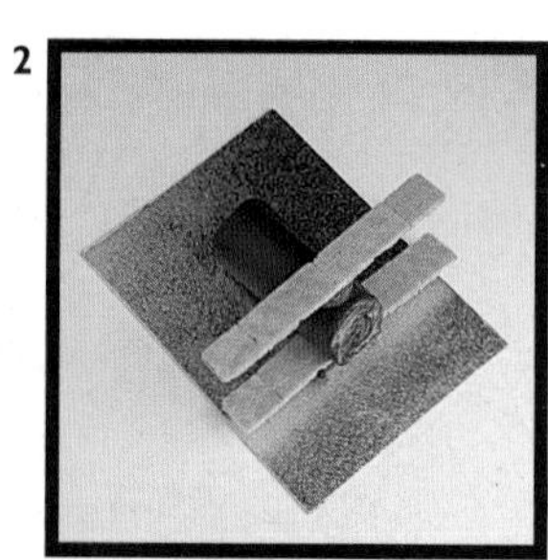

3

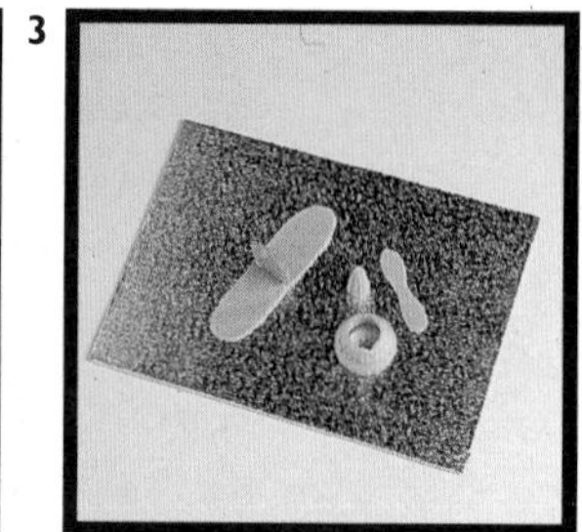

4

11

TREASURE ISLAND

4-egg Victoria sandwich mixture baked in a 20 × 30 cm (8 × 12 inch) Swiss roll tin and 600 ml (1 pint) basin
•
100 g (4 oz) vanilla butter icing
•
225 g (8 oz) green butter icing
•
green desiccated coconut
•
fine demerara sugar
•
1 Milky Way
•
dolly mixtures
•
liquorice allsorts
•
pink, gold and silver balls
•
Matchmakers
•
melted chocolate
•
50 g (2 oz) yellow royal icing
•
chopped blue jelly

1 For the island, cut the rectangular cake to shape as shown.
2 Place the cut pieces into position. Invert the basin cake and position at the top of the island to form a hill, sticking it on with icing. Trim the corners of the cake. Shape the land round the inlet and use for the long slope on the top.
3 Coat the sides of the cake with vanilla butter icing to resemble cliffs.
4 Spread green butter icing over the top of the cake and sprinkle with green coconut.
5 Spread a little vanilla butter icing on the board by the inlet and sprinkle with demerara sugar to look like sand.
6 Cut the top off the Milky Way with a sharp knife. Scoop out a little of cake and half bury the treasure chest. Fill with sweets and pink, gold and silver balls. Replace the lid.
7 Insert a liquorice allsort in the side of the hill for the entrance to a sweet mine. Make the fort and cannons with Matchmakers and melted chocolate (see page 116). If liked, make a hut using a Milky Way with chocolate thin mint crisp roof. Pipe a path from the fort to the inlet with yellow royal icing. Simply cut a liquorice comfit in half lengthways to make canoes and put on the beach or make out of moulding icing.
8 Decorate with flag poles, palm trees and boats, if liked. Surround the island with chopped blue jelly.

STEP

1

2
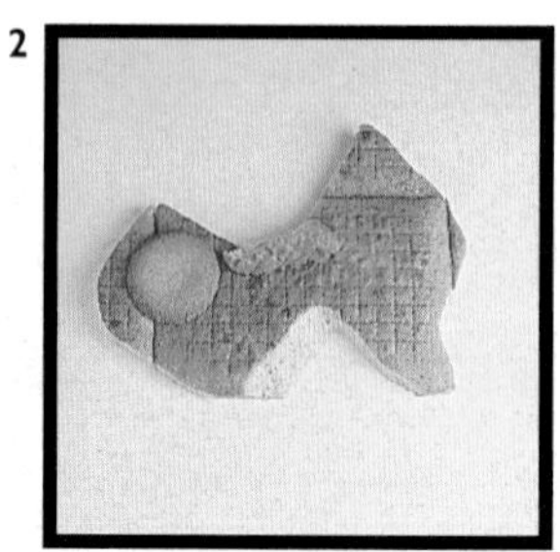

5
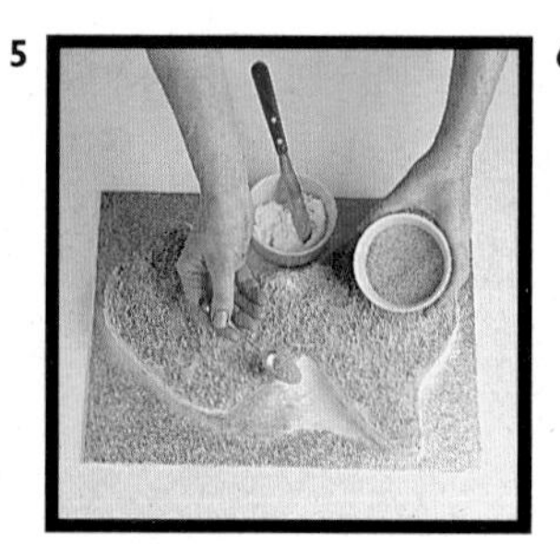

6
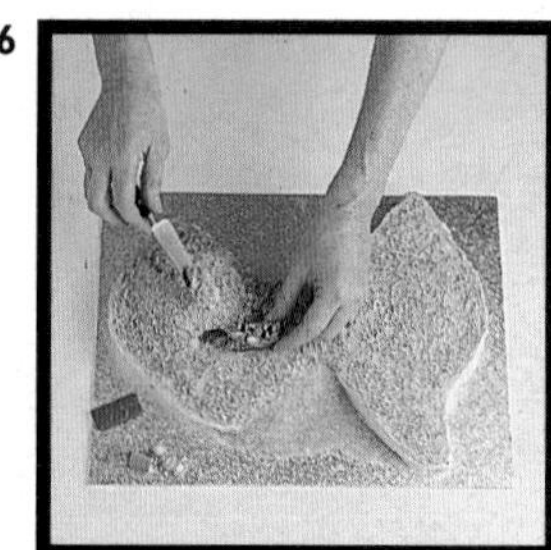

WICKED WITCH

4-egg Victoria sandwich mixture baked in an 18 cm (7 inch) shallow square tin and 18 × 28 cm (7 × 11 inch) oblong tin
•
100 g (4 oz) marzipan
•
175 g (6 oz) black butter icing
•
175 g (6 oz) green butter icing
•
1 white peppermint
•
red food colouring
•
black food colouring
•
liquorice comfits
•
liquorice strip
•
red piping gel
•
liquorice laces

1 Place the cakes together on a cake board and cut the hat and face outline as shown.
2 Cut the nose and hat brim as shown from sponge trimmings from the hat.
3 Roll out the marzipan and cut out stars and crescents.
4 Ice the hat with black butter icing and the face with green butter icing. Smooth the black and green icing evenly using a palette knife.
5 Paint the white mint with red food colouring to simulate a bloodshot eye, then paint a black pupil in the centre.
6 Cut liquorice comfit teeth and insert in the mouth. Place the eye in position and cut an eyelash from the liquorice strip. Pipe on some spots of red piping gel.
7 Place the marzipan stars and crescents on the hat. Arrange black liquorice laces as hair. Place the eyelash in position and pipe red gel around the lower half of the eye and around the lips.

STEP

1
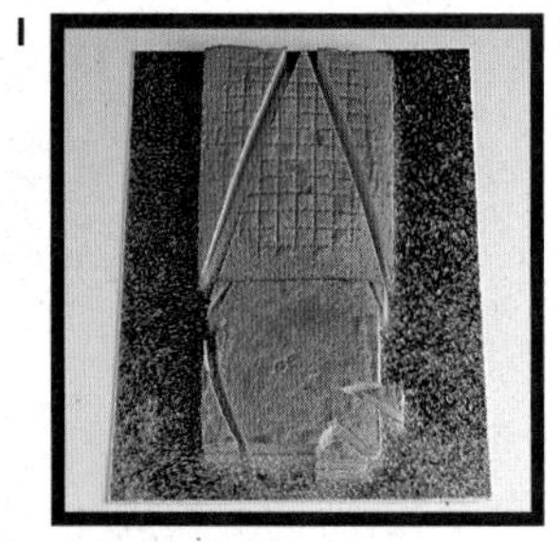

2
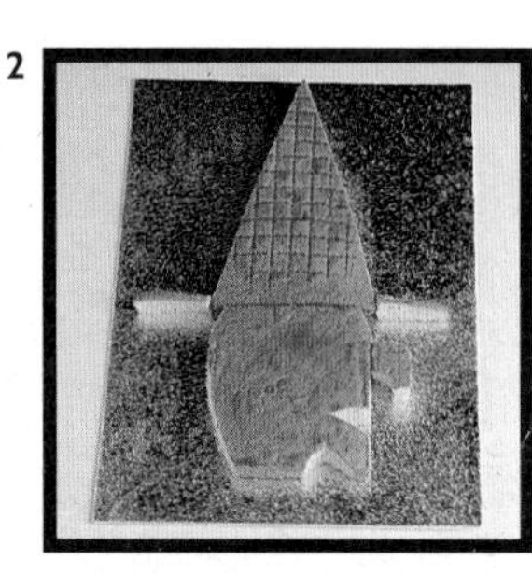

3

6
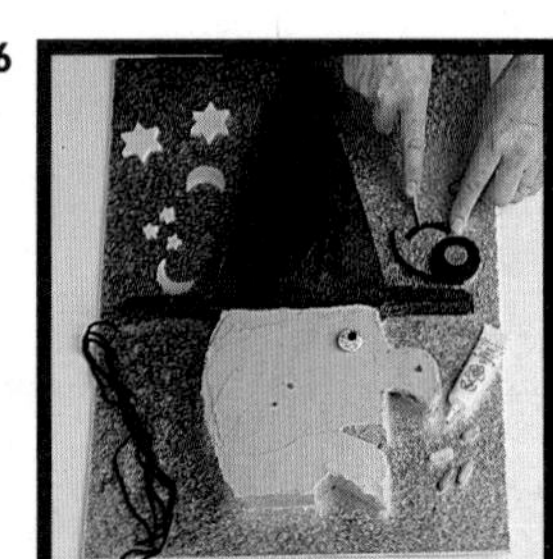

TANKER

I bought oblong chocolate Madeira cake
•
225 g (8 oz) melted chocolate
•
liquorice strip
•
black and red liquorice laces
•
I chocolate Swiss roll
•
4 mini chocolate coated Swiss rolls
•
50 g (2 oz) white moulding icing
•
wafers
•
chocolate beans
•
2 red fizzy lances
•
100 g (4 oz) red royal icing
•
assorted sweets

1 Cut two-thirds from the chocolate Madeira cake and dip in melted chocolate. Leave to dry, then stand upright on the cut surface on a cake board for the cab. Cut two 2.5 cm (1 inch) pieces of liquorice strip and stick into the back of the cab with lengths of red and black liquorice laces for wires for the electrics.

2 Coat the long Swiss roll in melted chocolate, leave to dry.

3 Lay the Swiss roll on top of three mini Swiss rolls on the cake board behind the cab.

4 Cut the ends from a mini Swiss roll and stick on either side of the cab with melted chocolate.

5 Cut white moulding icing to shape and stick on the front of the cab and the sides for windows and doors. Cut wafers into strips for the running boards.

6 Cut chocolate beans in half and stick on top of the cab for lights. Cut liquorice strip to size and attach with icing for the bumper. Stick chocolate beans on the wheels and tank.

7 Using melted chocolate, stick the strips of wafer on the mini rolls for the running boards. Lay a red fizzy lance pipe on top.

8 Cut an oval shape from moulding icing and write a logo on it. Stick the oval on to the side of the cake. Use red royal icing and sweets to decorate.

Note: For simplicity, the cakes do not need to be coated in chocolate.

STEP 1

3

4

5

Esso

KATIE CATERPILLAR

2–3 Swiss rolls
•
100 g (4 oz) green butter icing
•
hundreds and thousands
•
100 g (4 oz) chocolate butter icing
•
chocolate vermicelli
•
225 g (8 oz) green moulding icing
•
green food colouring
•
1 large truffle (see page 13)
•
2 lollies
•
2 large round peppermints
•
chocolate beans
•
liquorice comfits

1 Cut the Swiss rolls into 3 cm (1¼ inch) wide pieces.
2 Coat half the pieces with green butter icing and shake in hundreds and thousands to coat completely.
3 Coat the remaining pieces with chocolate butter icing and shake in vermicelli to coat completely. Leave to dry.
4 Roll out the green moulding icing, then cut into leaf shapes. Mark in veins with the back of a knife and paint with green food colouring. Lay the leaves on a cake board.
5 Lay the sections alternately on the leaves with a truffle at one end for the head.
6 Insert two lollies for feelers, peppermints for the eyes and chocolate beans for the mouth.
7 Decorate the caterpillar with chocolate beans and use liquorice comfits for legs. Paint eyes on to the peppermints, if liked.

STEP
1

2

3
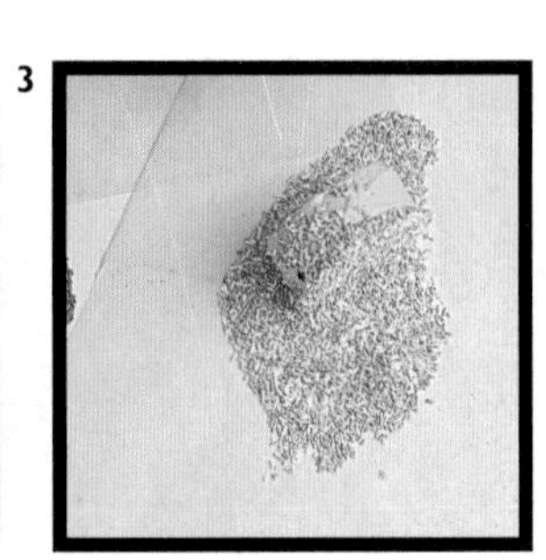
4
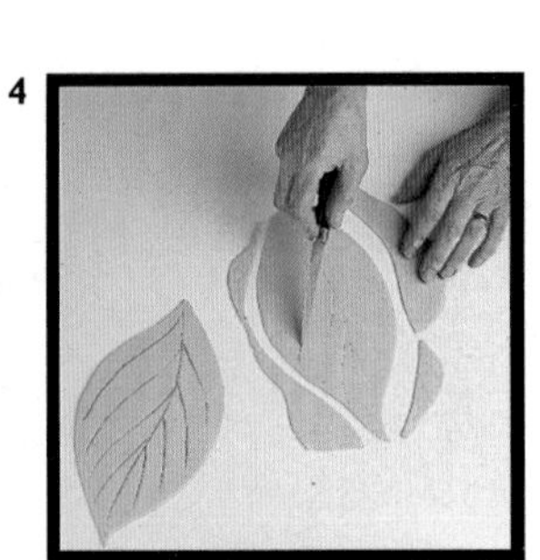

TEDDY BEAR

5-egg Madeira cake mixture baked in a 900 ml (1½ pint) and 600 ml (1 pint) basins and 18 cm (7 inch) sandwich tin

•

255 g (8 oz) coffee butter icing

•

3 long Matchmakers

•

50 g (2 oz) brown moulding icing

•

chocolate beans

•

liquorice laces

•

50 g (2 oz) red moulding icing

1 Cut a thin slice from the side of each basin cake to make a flat base. Cut a similar slice from the opposite side of the larger cake.

2 Cut ears, legs and arms from the sandwich cake as shown, then round them off.

3 Cut each leg to shape as shown.

4 Cut a nose from the slice cut off earlier, then trim to a round shape. Attach to the head with icing. Assemble the bear.

5 Using a 0.5 cm (¼ inch) wooden skewer, make a hole in the head and body. Insert a long Matchmaker to hold them together securely.

6 Coat the bear completely with coffee butter icing. Coat the ears and attach to the head.

7 Coat the arms with icing and attach to the cake using Matchmakers. Ice the legs and place in position. Rough up all the icing.

8 Put brown moulding icing pads on the feet and paws, chocolate beans for eyes and nose, and liquorice strips for the mouth and claws.

9 Make a scarf from the red moulding icing and tie around his neck (see page 34).

STEP

1

2

3

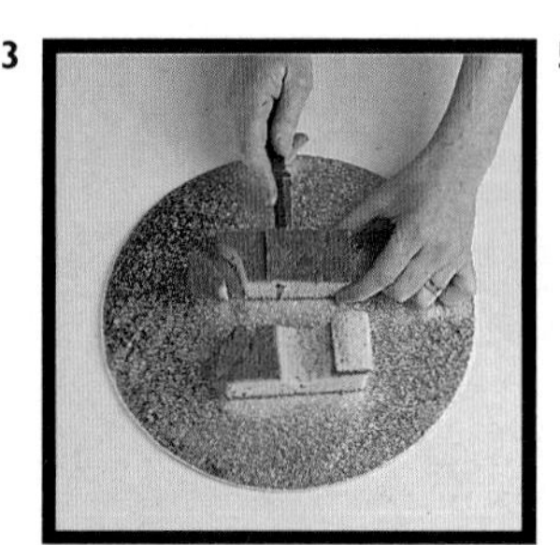

5

Methuen
Methuen

VALENTINE CAKE

3-egg Victoria sandwich mixture baked in a 20 cm (8 inch) deep heart shape tin
•
100 g (4 oz) butter icing
•
apricot glaze
•
450 g (1 lb) pink moulding icing
•
50 g (2 oz) white moulding icing
•
egg white
•
50 g (2 oz) pink royal icing

1 Cut the cake in half horizontally and sandwich with butter icing. Brush the cake with apricot glaze.
2 Roll out pink moulding icing and cut to a 25 cm (10 inch) heart shape. Lay the icing centrally over the cake and mould to fit, cutting off the excess.
3 Roll out the white moulding icing. Cut heart shapes from the white and some remaining pink moulding icing. Leave to dry.
4 Roll out pink moulding icing thinly and cut a 7.5 cm (3 inch) round using a fluted cutter. Cut out the centre with a plain cutter, then cut through the circle in one place.
5 With a cocktail stick, roll each flute to stretch the icing.
6 Lay the icing out in a line to make a frill.
7 Mark a scallop on the cake side using egg white. Lift up the frill and attach to the cake, pressing gently into position. Repeat with a further four frills.
8 Decorate the top of the frill with pink royal icing using a No 2 writing nozzle.
9 Arrange heart shapes on the cake.

Note: If liked, you can vary the shades of pink or use white for the frill and hearts.

STEP

3

5
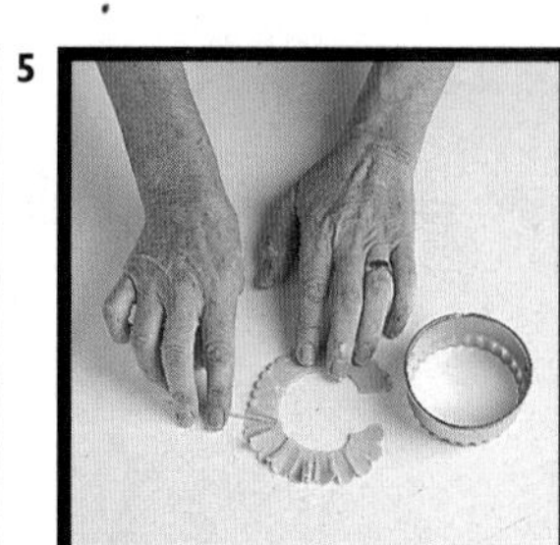

6
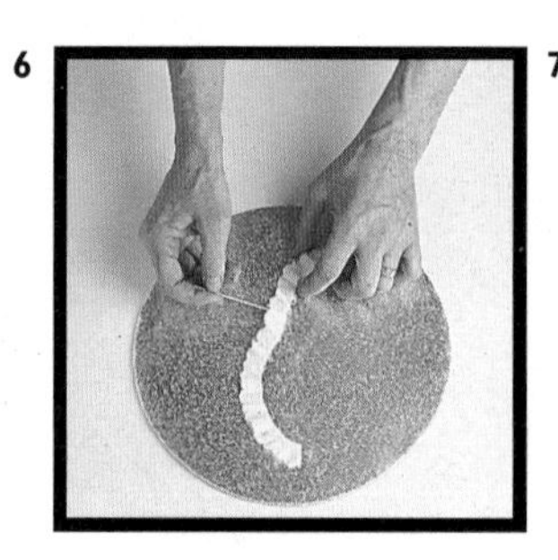

7
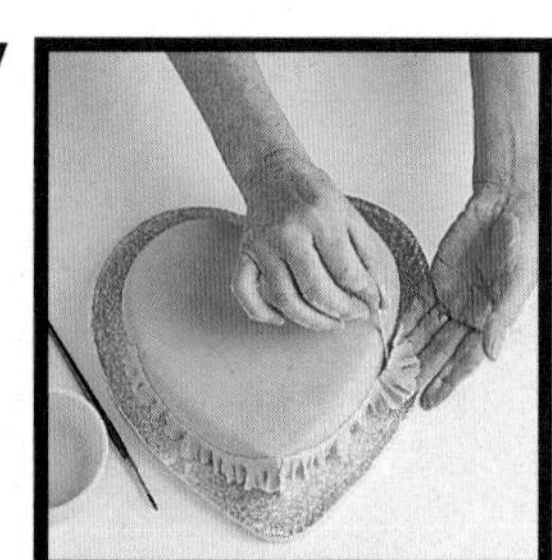

ROCKET

1 chocolate Swiss roll
•
350 g (12 oz) melted chocolate
•
wafers
•
chocolate thin mint crisps
•
1 ice cream cone
•
3 mini chocolate Swiss rolls
•
assorted sweets
•
50 g (2 oz) white royal icing
•
50 g (2 oz) red royal icing
•
liquorice allsorts

1 Coat the large Swiss roll with melted chocolate and leave to dry on an uncoated end.
2 Cut fins to shape from wafers and chocolate mint crisps. Dip the wafer fins and ice cream nose cone into melted chocolate, then set aside to dry.
3 Stand the coated Swiss roll on end on a cake board. Using melted chocolate, stick the three mini Swiss rolls into place at equal distances apart around the base of the large one, with the flat sides inwards.
4 Stick the nose cone in position with melted chocolate. Attach the coated wafer fins at the second stage and chocolate mint fins at the base.
5 Decorate with sweets and white and red piping as liked. Cut the number from liquorice allsorts and attach to the rocket with melted chocolate.

Note: To make the spaceman, see Space Ship on page 24.

STEP

2

3

4

5
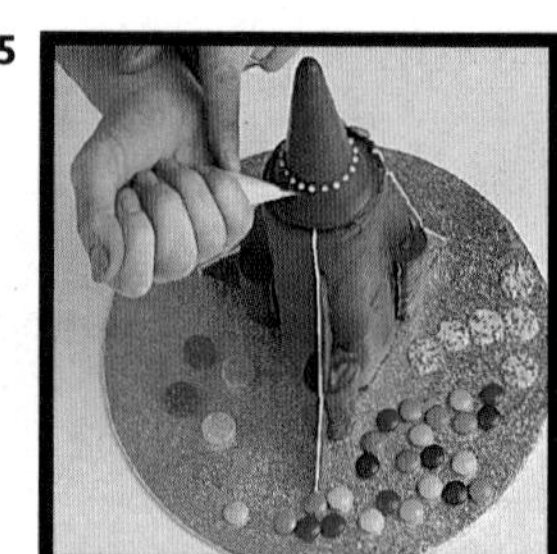

32

THATCHED COTTAGE

5-egg Madeira cake mixture baked in a 20 cm (8 inch) square tin
•
225 g (8 oz) vanilla butter icing
•
liquorice strips
•
wafers
•
wafer biscuits
•
100 g (4 oz) coffee butter icing
•
50 g (2 oz) white royal icing
•
mini liquorice allsorts
•
cotton wool
•
100 g (4 oz) green butter icing
•
hundreds and thousands

1 Cut a third off the cake lengthways and level the top if necessary.
2 Cut the smaller piece diagonally as shown and put the two short sides together to form the roof.
3 Stick the roof together with icing, then attach to the larger cake with icing.
4 Spread the cake with vanilla butter icing and place on a cake board.
5 Cut out strips of liquorice and attach to the cake to form beams.
6 Cut out wafers for doors and windows. Cut wafer biscuits to shape for chimney and dormer windows. Stick them into position with icing.
7 Coat the chimney and sides of dormer windows with vanilla butter icing.
8 Coat the roof with coffee butter icing and fork up to resemble a thatched roof.
9 Pipe the windows with white royal icing. Stick window sills and chimney pots into position. Add some cotton wool for smoke. Spread the cake board with green butter icing and sprinkle hundreds and thousands over the path.

STEP

1

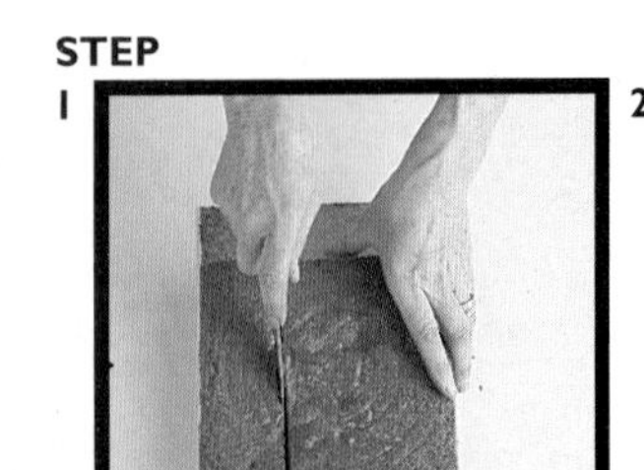

2

3

6

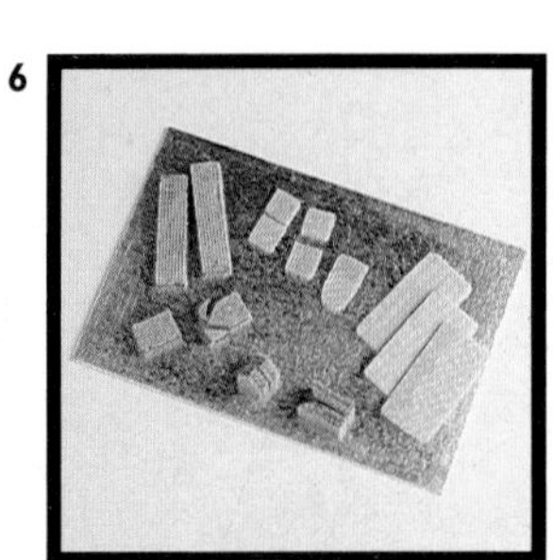

BIG RED BUS

9-egg Victoria sandwich mixture baked in three 18 × 28cm (7 × 11 inch) tins
•
450 g (1 lb) red butter icing
•
wafers
•
white edible wafer
•
50 g (2 oz) chocolate butter icing
•
4 round chocolate biscuits
•
chocolate beans
•
liquorice strip
•
1 Matchmaker
•
100 g (4 oz) red royal icing

1 From the underside of each of two cakes, cut two 6.5 cm (2½ inch) rounds 0.5 cm (¼ inch) deep. From the widest points of each round cut straight lines, 0.5 cm (¼ inch) deep, down to the edge of the cake and cut out as shown to form the wheel arches.
2 Cut out an oblong from the bottom right of one cake 9 × 5 cm (3½ × 2 inches) to form the entrance. Cut a 4 cm (1½ inch) square from the middle of the other end to form the engine recess.
3 Sandwich the three cakes together with red butter icing ensuring that the wheel arches correspond. Trim the edges to straighten, then stand the bus on a cake board. Cut rounded edges at the front and back at the top of the cake.
4 Cut the windows and radiator grill to shape from wafers. Cut the advertising strip, number plate and direction boards from white edible wafer. Set aside.
5 Using a palette knife, coat the bus, except the entrance, smoothly with red butter icing. Spread the chocolate butter icing in the entrance. Place the chocolate biscuit wheels into place in the wheel arches.
6 Push into position the wafer and edible white wafer cut outs, chocolate bean lights and other decorations. Stick liquorice strip around the wheel arches and base of bus.
7 Cut out the entrance platform from a wafer and cut out another slightly smaller all round. Push into position so that the smaller piece does not show. Insert the Matchmaker in the top of the entrance and rest the other end on the platform. Pipe red royal icing around the windows.

Note: In order to sandwich the cakes together properly, slice off the rounded tops of cakes that have risen too much.

Remember that the bus is right hand drive; the entrance must be cut from the right edge and the engine recess from the left edge of the cake. Make sure you cut the wheel arches on the second cake with the front wheel at the right of the cake so they will line up when you sandwich the cakes together.

STEP 1

2

3

4

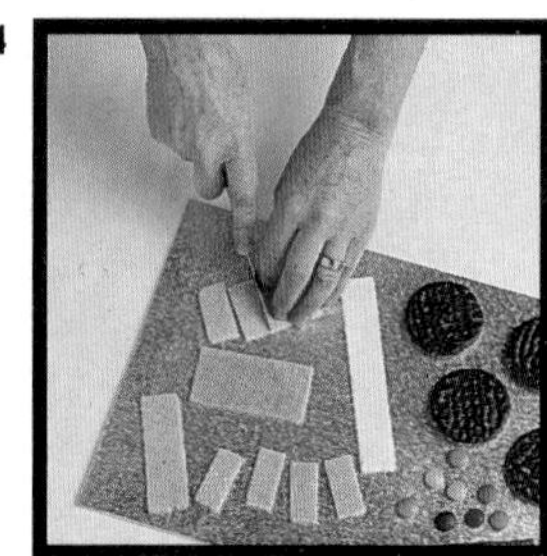

69A BIG BEN
'Les Miserables' THE PALACE THEATRE
BOX OFFICE
69A
TIM 1

FREDDIE FROG

4-egg Madeira cake mixture baked in a 900 ml (1½ pint) basin and 600 ml (1 pint) basin
•
4 sponge fingers
•
225 g (8 oz) green butter icing
•
50 g (2 oz) pink butter icing
•
225 g (8 oz) green moulding icing
•
black food colouring
•
2 peppermint sweets
•
chopped blue jelly

1 For the base of the head, remove a piece from the small cake as shown.
2 Turn the cake round and cut through to form the mouth.
3 Cut the removed piece of cake in half for haunches and shape the sponge fingers for legs. Assemble the frog on the cake board, using the large cake for the body.
4 Coat the head with green butter icing, using pink butter icing for the mouth. Coat the legs and body with green butter icing.
5 Roll out the green moulding icing and cut out webbed feet. Stick on the end of the legs with a little green icing. Use the remaining moulding icing to make some lily leaves, then leave them to dry completely before using.
6 Paint black food colouring on the mints for eyes and stick into position with icing.
7 Surround the frog with chopped blue jelly and float the lily leaves on top.

STEP

1
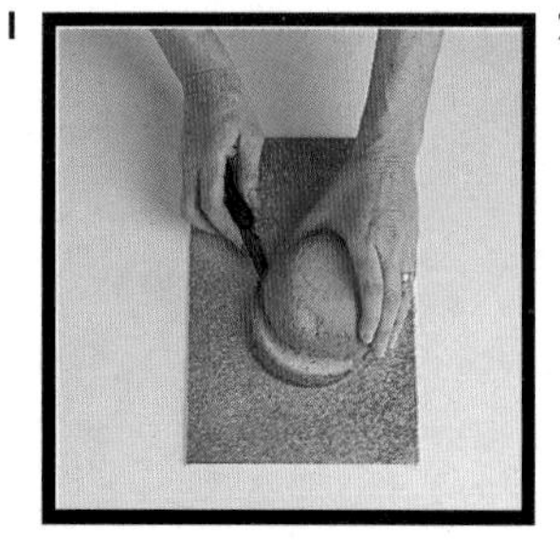

2
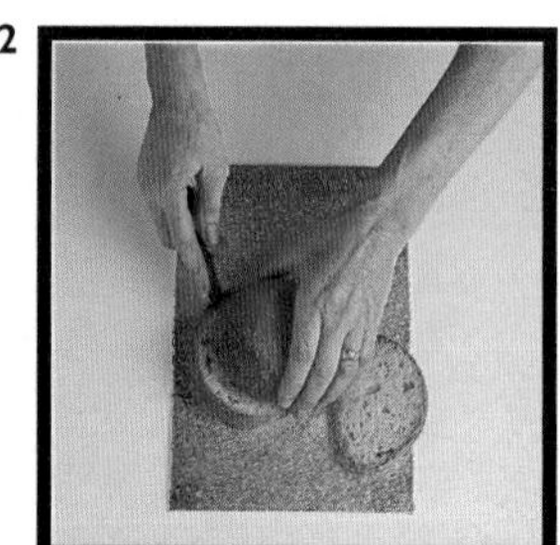

3
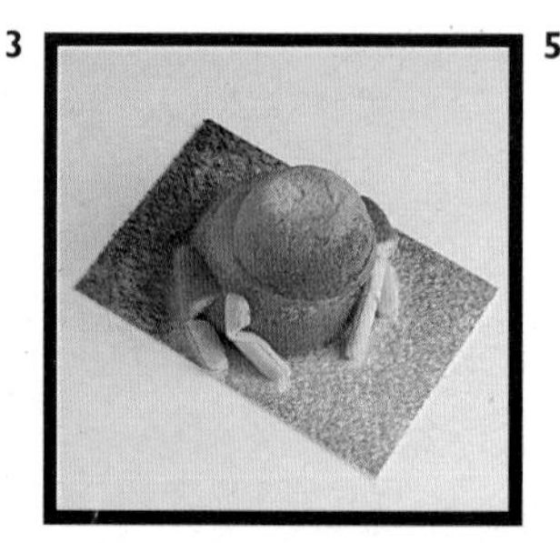

5
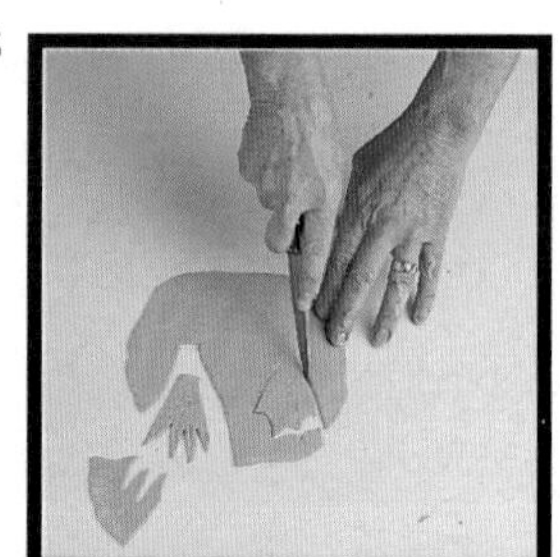

BOXING RING

3-egg Madeira cake mixture baked in an 18 cm (7 inch) deep square tin
•
100 g (4 oz) chocolate butter icing
•
apricot glaze
•
225 g (8 oz) yellow moulding icing
•
225 g (8 oz) brown moulding icing
•
Matchmakers
•
red liquorice laces
•
50 g (2 oz) melted chocolate
•
4 liquorice comfits
•
2 plastic boxers
•
2 Rolos
•
50 g (2 oz) white moulding icing (optional)

1 Cut the cake in half horizontally and sandwich together with chocolate butter icing. Turn the cake upside down to give a flat surface. Brush the cake with apricot glaze.
2 Roll out the yellow moulding icing, cut out an 18 cm (7 inch) square and cover the top of the cake.
3 Roll out the chocolate moulding icing to two long strips the same width as the depth of the cake and wrap around the sides of the cake.
4 Using a 0.5 cm (¼ inch) wooden skewer, make deep holes in each corner of the cake. Insert the Matchmakers.
5 Join two lengths of red liquorice laces by heating the ends and squeezing together.
6 Put dabs of melted chocolate on the outside of the Matchmakers and attach the liquorice laces to make the rails.
7 Attach the liquorice comfits to the inside of the Matchmakers with melted chocolate.
8 Place the boxers in position. Put Rolo stools in the two corners. Arrange white moulding icing towels over the rails, if liked. You can even make a bucket.

STEP

2
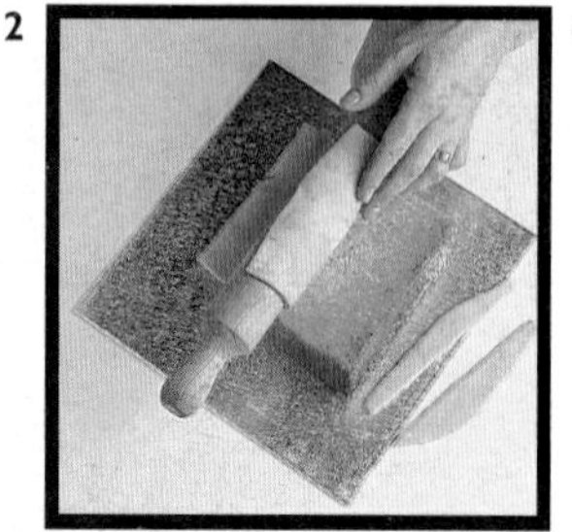

4

6

7

CHUFFA TRAIN

1 bought oblong chocolate Madeira cake
•
225 g (8 oz) melted chocolate
•
6 mini chocolate coated Swiss rolls
•
1 chocolate coated Swiss roll
•
50 g (2 oz) white moulding icing
•
blackjacks
•
liquorice comfits
•
chocolate beans
•
1 Rolo
•
6 iced ring biscuits
•
2 long Matchmakers
•
100 g (4 oz) red royal icing

1 Cut a third off the Madeira cake. Dip each piece into melted chocolate to coat completely and leave to set on greaseproof paper.
2 Position five mini Swiss rolls on a cake board and lay the Swiss roll and two pieces of Madeira cake on top.
3 Roll out the white moulding icing and cut windows to shape. Brush with melted chocolate and stick into position.
4 Cut two-thirds off a mini Swiss roll for the funnel and attach to the boiler with melted chocolate.
5 Cut the blackjacks into cubes for coal and place on the tender.
6 Cut the ends off four liquorice comfits. Stand two in moulding icing to balance. Dip two chocolate beans in a little melted chocolate and attach to comfits. When dry, place in position for buffers. Stick the remaining comfits on top of the cab. Stick a chocolate bean on a Rolo for a funnel and position on top of the boiler with melted chocolate.
7 Lay two rows of three iced biscuits side by side. Brush two Matchmakers with melted chocolate and attach one to each row of biscuits. When dry, attach to the sides of the engine.
8 Decorate with red royal icing as liked.

Note: For a simpler train there is no need to dip the cake in chocolate. Add cotton wool smoke to the funnel.

STEP

1

2
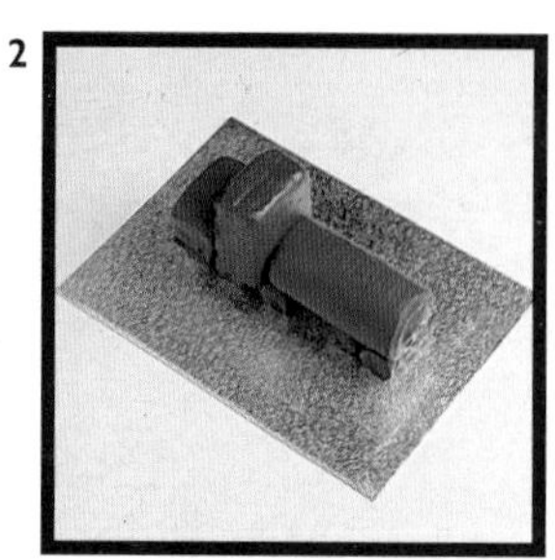

6

7

DINO DINOSAUR

4-egg Victoria sandwich mixture baked in two 20 cm (8 inch) sandwich tins
•
225 g (8 oz) green butter icing
•
1 long Matchmaker
•
chocolate thin mint crisps
•
chocolate beans
•
50 g (2 oz) white royal icing
•
candy sticks
•
100 g (4 oz) coffee butter icing
•
chopped blue jelly

1 Cut one cake in half and shape both halves to form the legs and stomach.
2 Cut a third from the other cake. Cut a curved 2.5 cm (1 inch) wide strip, 7.5 cm (3 inches) long, from the outside edge of the cake for the neck and head. From the large piece of cake, cut out a curved shape to form the chest, reserving the small piece for the tail.
3 Sandwich the three cakes together with butter icing with the chest piece in the middle, allowing it to protrude 2.5 cm (1 inch) at the rear end. Place the tail in position.
4 Attach the head to the body with a Matchmaker.
5 Coat the cake completely in the green butter icing. Cut large and small triangles from the chocolate thin mint crisps. Place the large triangles along the spine and smaller triangles on the neck and tail. Put chocolate beans in position for the eyes. Pipe teeth using white royal icing, then stick on two fangs cut from candy sticks. Add chocolate bean claws to the base of each leg.
6 Ice rocks, made from pieces of cakes, with coffee butter icing and place on the board. Apply plants with green butter icing or use angelica. Surround the dinosaur with chopped blue jelly.

STEP

1

2
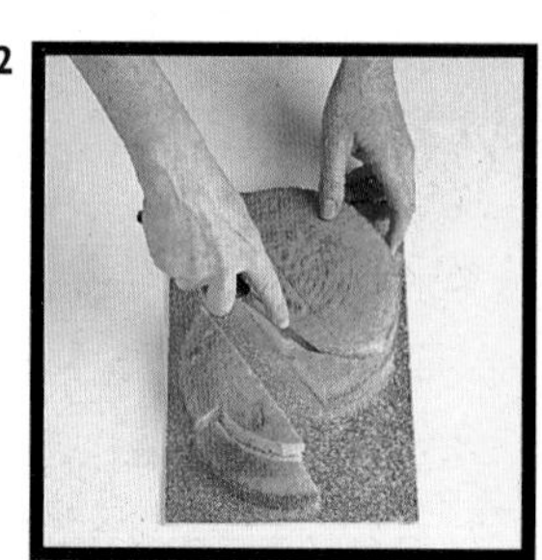

3
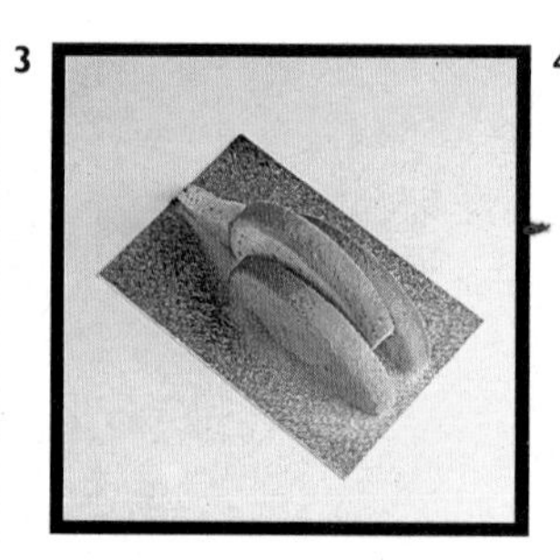

4
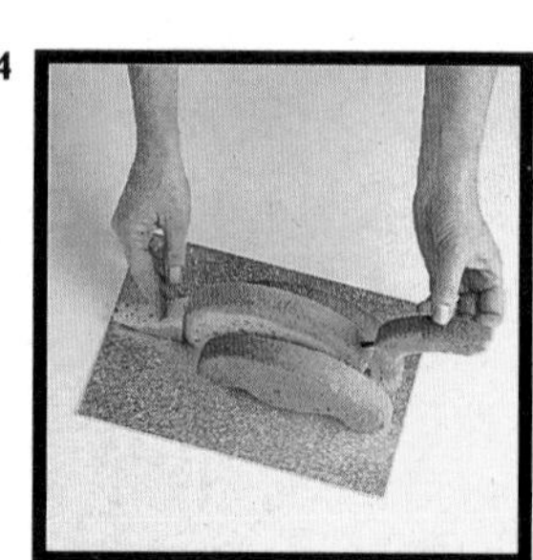

TOADSTOOL AND GOBLINS

4-egg Madeira cake mixture baked in a 2.3 litre (4 pint) basin and 793 g (1 lb 12 oz) can
•
100 g (4 oz) chocolate butter icing
•
apricot glaze
•
350 g (12 oz) red moulding icing
•
2 mini chocolate coated Swiss rolls
•
4 chocolate coated teacakes
•
100 g (4 oz) green moulding icing
•
50 g (2 oz) pink moulding icing
•
100 g (4 oz) red royal icing
•
liquorice allsorts
•
100 g (4 oz) green butter icing

1 Spread the cylindrical cake with chocolate butter icing, making it thicker towards the base. Place upright on a cake board for the stalk.

2 Brush the basin cake with apricot glaze. Roll out the red moulding icing into a round and place over the glazed cake. Fold the surplus icing underneath.

3 Place the cake centrally on top of the stalk. To make small toadstools, cut the Swiss rolls in half and stick a teacake on top of each half with icing.

4 Use both of the moulding icings to make the goblins and decorate them with red royal icing. Pipe dots on the small toadstools with red royal icing. Slice the liquorice allsorts and put on the large toadstool.

5 Spread green butter icing on the cake board and rough up with a palette knife. Put the goblins, small toadstools and any creatures you may like to make or buy in position.

STEP

1

2

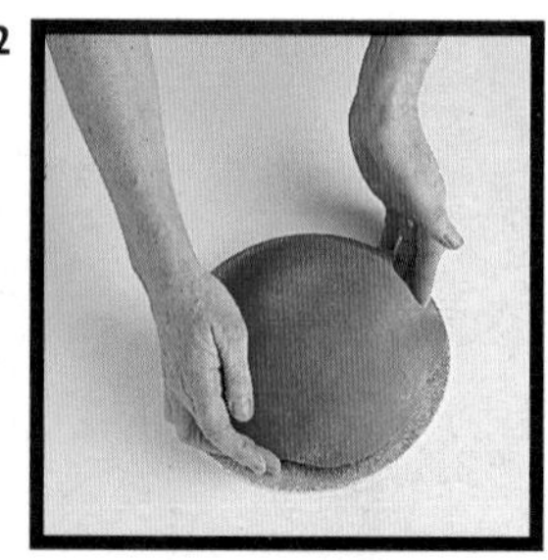

3

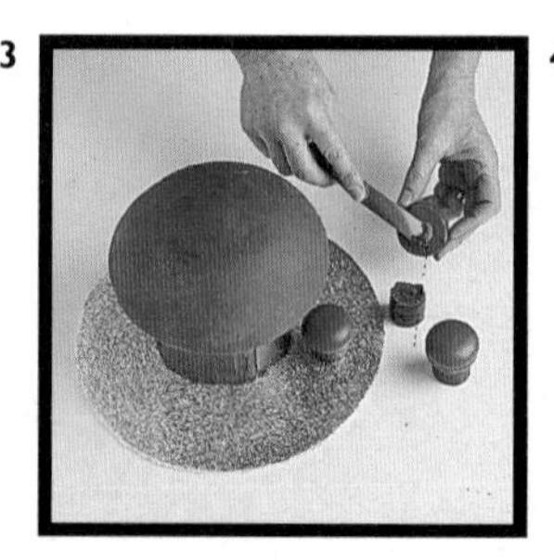

4

SAMMY SPIDER

3-egg Madeira cake mixture baked in a 1 litre (2 pint) basin
•
225 g (8 oz) chocolate butter icing
•
chocolate vermicelli
•
25 g (1oz) melted chocolate
•
10 chocolate beans
•
1 chocolate coated teacake
•
strawberry flavoured fizzy lances or thick red liquorice
•
12 long Matchmakers
•
225 g (8 oz) green royal icing
•
50 g (2 oz) chocolate royal icing

1 Cut the cake in half horizontally and sandwich together with some of the chocolate butter icing. Completely cover the cake with chocolate icing and sprinkle with chocolate vermicelli. Leave to dry.
2 Using melted chocolate, stick two chocolate beans on to the teacake for eyes and two strips of red liquorice on to the base of the cake for feelers. Leave to set.
3 Break four long Matchmakers in half and stick each half to a long Matchmaker at right angles with melted chocolate, then leave on greaseproof paper to set.
4 Ice a cake board with green royal icing or ice a round of icing on the board. Pipe circles of chocolate royal icing, then use a sharp knife to mark the web. Leave to dry.
5 Lay the body of the spider on the web. Make eight holes in the cake towards the top. Insert the legs, resting the feet on chocolate beans using a little melted chocolate to attach.
6 Attach the head to the body with a Matchmaker and a little icing to secure in position. Alternatively, stand the head on the board instead of attaching it further up the body.

Note: Use royal icing for the web so that it sets firmly enough to stand the spider on top without smudging it.

STEP

1

2

3

4
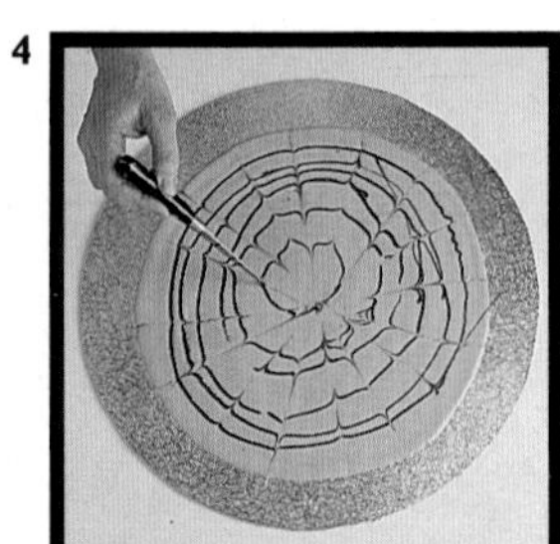

BUZZY BUMBLE BEE

3-egg Madeira cake mixture baked in a 900 ml (1½ pint) and 450 ml (¾ pint) basin
•
100 g (4 oz) yellow butter icing
•
apricot glaze
•
100 g (4 oz) brown moulding icing
•
100 g (4 oz) chocolate butter icing
•
yellow desiccated coconut
•
chocolate vermicelli
•
2 sheets rice paper
•
brown food colouring
•
7 Matchmakers
•
25 g (1 oz) melted chocolate
•
2 chocolate beans
•
2 liquorice allsorts

1 Trim the smaller cake as shown. Cut both cakes in half horizontally and sandwich together with butter icing, then lay them flat side down on a cake board. Brush the smaller cake with apricot glaze.
2 Roll out the brown moulding icing to a 20 cm (8 inch) round and lay over the glazed cake. Fold the icing underneath, trimming off any excess icing.
3 Spread alternate stripes of yellow and chocolate butter icings over the larger cake. Sprinkle yellow coconut over the yellow icing and chocolate vermicelli over the chocolate icing.
4 Cut wing shapes from the rice paper. Paint lightly with brown food colouring for veins.
5 Cut Matchmakers and stick together at an angle using melted chocolate to make legs. For the two feelers, halve a Matchmaker and stick a chocolate bean on top of each. Lay them on grease-proof paper to dry.
6 Attach the wings with melted chocolate. Make holes in the cakes, then insert the legs and feelers. Stick on liquorice allsorts with icing for eyes. Pipe a yellow mouth.

STEP
1
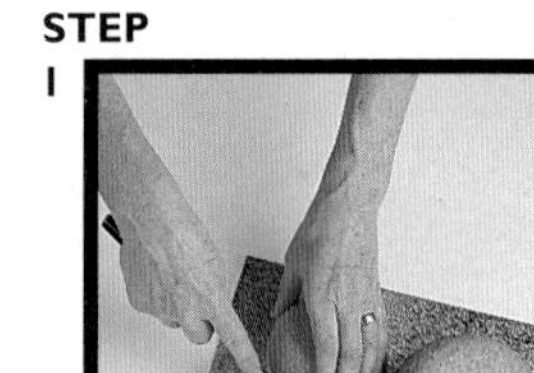
2
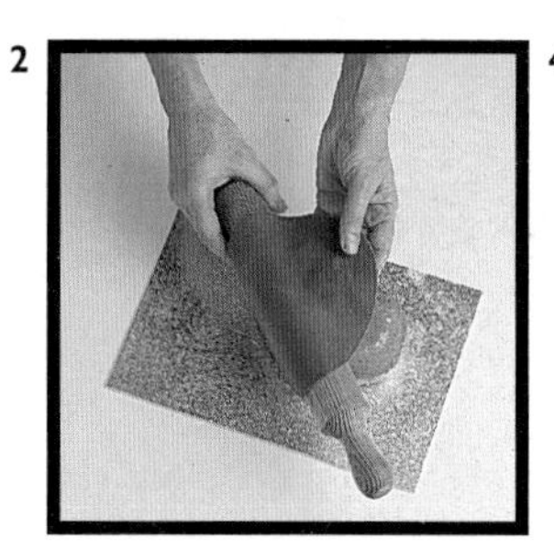
4
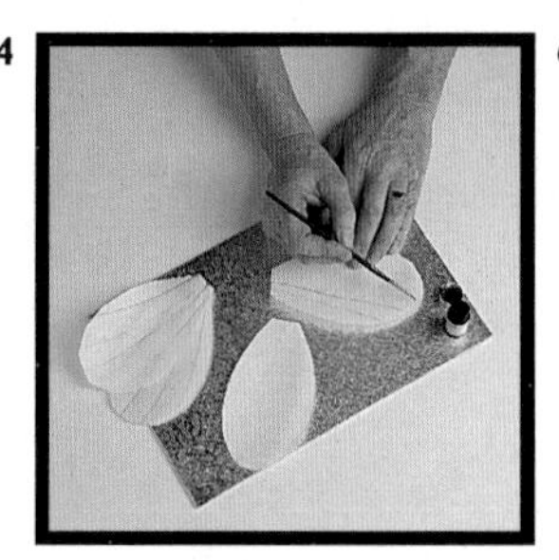
6
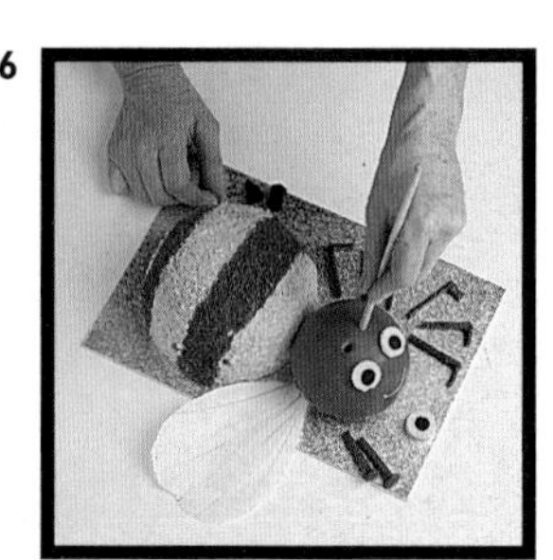

MAN ON THE MOON

4 ice cream cones
•
5-egg Madeira cake mixture baked in a 4 litre (7 pint) basin
•
225 g (8 oz) soft white icing
•
silver balls
•
candy sticks
•
4 marshmallows
•
sandwich wafer biscuits
•
25 g (1 oz) melted chocolate
•
iced ring biscuit
•
dolly mixtures
•
50 g (2 oz) red marzipan
•
15 g (½ oz) white marzipan
•
chocolate bean
•
liquorice allsort
•
liquorice lace

1 Cut the cones to shape and place on the cake as shown.
2 Cover the cake and cones with white icing and sprinkle silver balls over the craters.
3 To make the buggy, first make the front axle assembly by sticking a candy stick into the middle of a marshmallow. Stick another marshmallow on the other end. Repeat for the back axle.
4 Cut two sandwich wafer biscuits in half horizontally and lay one half over the two candy stick axles. Stick a candy stick on to the other half of the wafer biscuit with melted chocolate as shown, to make a solar panel. Cut another wafer biscuit into a rounded seat back as shown. Cut an iced ring biscuit in half for rear mud guards.
5 Assemble the buggy as shown, sticking in position with melted chocolate. Decorate with sweets for the seat, engines and lights.
6 Mould a spaceman from red and white marzipan and put a chocolate bean over the face for a mask. Attach a liquorice allsort backpack and liquorice lace to his helmet for a life line.

STEP

1

3

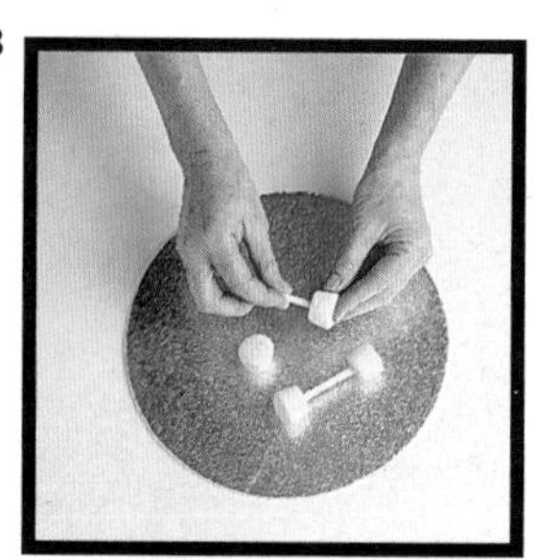

4

5

VEGETABLE PATCH

4-egg Victoria sandwich mixture baked in a 20 × 30 cm (8 × 12 inch) Swiss roll tin
•
225 g (8 oz) chocolate butter icing
•
chocolate flakes
•
225 g (8 oz) green butter icing
•
green desiccated coconut
•
Matchmakers
•
melted chocolate
•
green fizzy lances
•
50 g (2 oz) red royal icing
•
moulding icing vegetables (see page 9)
•
sugar flowers

1 Ice the sides of the cake with chocolate butter icing and coat with chocolate flakes.
2 Spread a 2.5 cm (1 inch) border of green butter icing around the top of the cake, across the middle and to divide one half into quarters. Sprinkle with green coconut.
3 Carefully spread the insides of the squares with chocolate butter icing and sprinkle with chocolate flakes.
4 For the bean poles, cut four Matchmakers in half, shape into V's and stick at the apex with melted chocolate. Leave to set.
5 Stick a Matchmaker along the top to join the bean poles together.
6 Stick the bean poles into one of the earthed areas. Cut green fizzy lances in half lengthways and drape over the bean poles. Pipe red flowers on the runner beans.
7 Plant vegetables moulded from coloured moulding icing or use appropriately coloured sweets instead. Plant flowers made from sweets or piped royal icing in the remaining patch.

Note: A wheelbarrow can be made from chocolate thin mint crisps, Matchmakers and melted chocolate.

STEP

2

3

4

5

WINNIE WHALE

4-egg Madeira cake mixture baked in a 20 × 30 cm (8 × 12 inch) Swiss roll tin and 600 ml (1 pint) basin
•
apricot glaze
•
300 g (10 oz) pale blue moulding icing
•
100 g (4 oz) dark blue butter icing
•
15 ml (1 tbsp) vanilla butter icing
•
50 g (2 oz) white or pink moulding icing
•
egg white
•
2 pink liquorice allsorts
•
1 candle
•
black food colouring
•
2 mint sweets

1 Brush the basin cake with apricot glaze. Roll out the pale blue moulding icing to a round, place over the cake and mould to shape. Trim off the excess icing.

2 Use the trimmings to make a tail as shown and leave overnight to dry, draped over a bowl.

3 Lay the flat cake on a board and spread the top and sides with dark blue butter icing. Dab on vanilla butter icing in places to resemble 'white horses'.

4 Roll out the white or pink moulding icing and cut out a mouth to the preferred shape. Brush with egg white and attach to the whale.

5 When the tail has dried, stick into position on the sea with butter icing.

6 Cut two thin pink slices from the liquorice allsorts and make thin cuts along one side for eyelashes. Bend into a curve and stick on to the cake with egg white. With black food colouring, paint pupils on the mint sweets for eyes and attach with a little icing. Put a candle in the top and light.

STEP

1

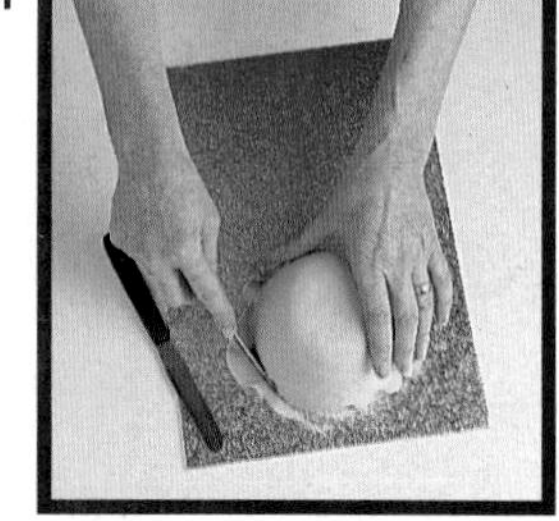

2

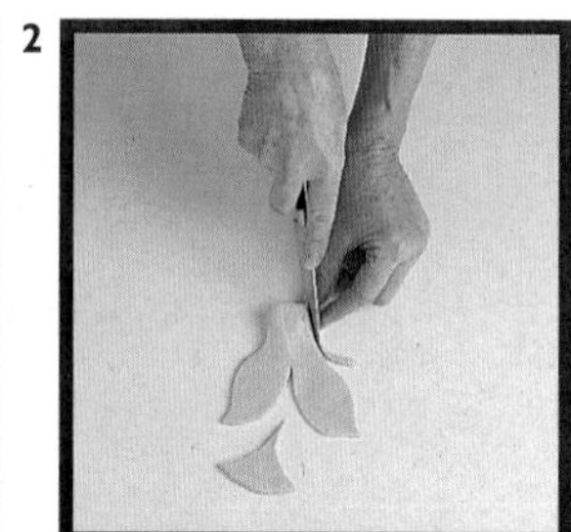

3

4

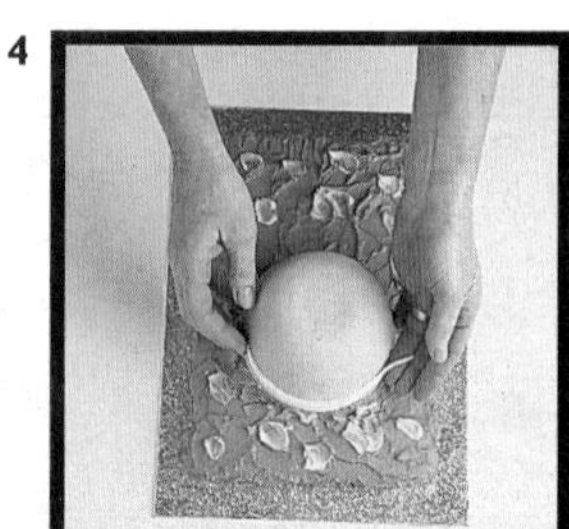

CRICKET BAT

2-egg Victoria sandwich mixture baked in a 20 × 30 cm (8 × 12 inch) Swiss roll tin
•
100 g (4 oz) chocolate butter icing
•
350 g (12 oz) coffee moulding icing
•
brown food colouring
•
3 chocolate coated mini Swiss rolls
•
apricot glaze
•
100 g (4 oz) chocolate moulding icing
•
50 g (2 oz) red royal icing
•
1 large chocolate truffle (see page 13)
•
100 g (4 oz) red moulding icing
•
50 g (2 oz) white royal icing

1 Cut the cake in half lengthways and sandwich together with chocolate butter icing.
2 Cut off both sides diagonally from the centre to half way down the top cake.
3 Cut off a similar section at both ends, starting 5 cm (2 inches) in from the ends. Round off the shoulder and foot of the bat.
4 Roll out the coffee moulding icing to a rectangle measuring 16 × 35 cm (6½ × 14 inches). Lay the icing over the cake and cut to shape. Mould to fit the bat and put on a board.
5 Make a slight 'v' shape indent at the top of the bat in the icing with the back of a knife. Paint the triangular area using brown food colouring.
6 Brush the mini Swiss rolls with apricot glaze. Roll out the chocolate moulding icing to a rectangle measuring 10 × 20 cm (4 × 8 inches). Use to coat the Swiss rolls, pressed together. Place the handle in position on the board.
7 Write on the cake in red royal icing.
8 To make a cricket ball, cover the truffle in red moulding icing and smooth round. Pipe the stitching in white royal icing.

STEP

1

2
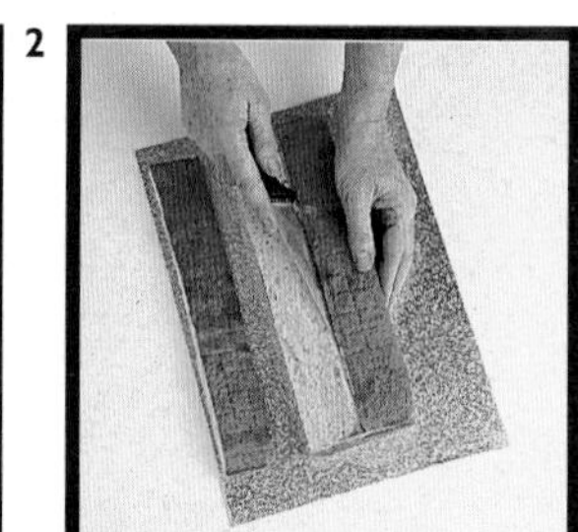

3
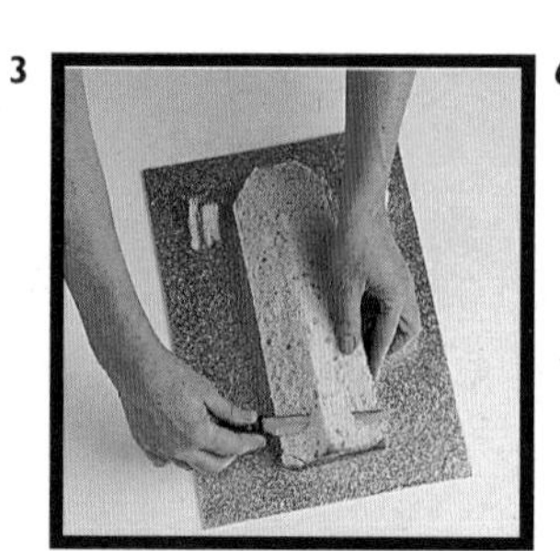

6
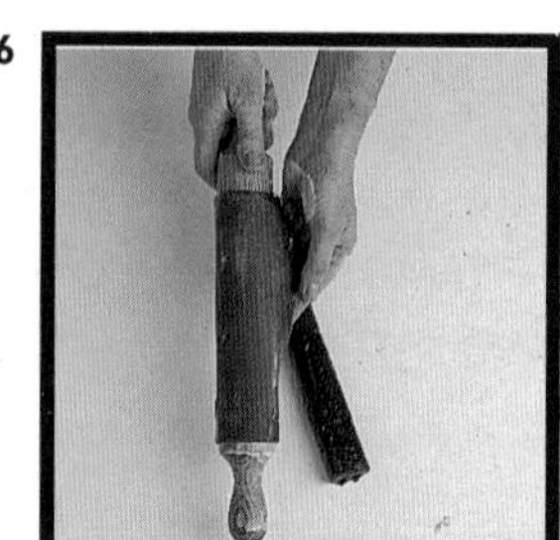

Happy
Birthday

WALKMAN

2 bought oblong Madeira cakes
•
100 g (4 oz) vanilla butter icing
•
apricot glaze
•
450 g (1 lb) yellow marzipan
•
liquorice allsorts
•
50 g (2 oz) white marzipan
•
50 g (2 oz) red royal icing
•
50 g (2 oz) black royal icing
•
2 liquorice catherine wheels
•
red liquorice laces
•
red fizzy lances

1 Trim the tops off the cakes, sandwich together with butter icing and brush with apricot glaze.

2 Roll out the yellow marzipan and cut out a rectangle measuring 38 × 15 cm (15 × 6 inches) and two oblongs measuring 12.5 × 6.5 cm (5 × 2½ inches). Lay the cake on the rectangle of marzipan and wrap around it. Place the oblongs of marzipan on the ends. Mould the joins together with a palette knife.

3 Cut two circles out of the marzipan on the front of the cake with a 1 cm (½ inch) round cutter and discard. Stick two liquorice allsorts in the spaces provided, with a little icing.

4 Cut out a small rectangle of yellow marzipan measuring 9 × 5 cm (3½ × 2 inches). Insert a similar sized white marzipan rectangle for the cassette window.

5 Stick liquorice allsorts in the top and sides to form switches, removing the marzipan first as shown in step 3 for a neater finish.

6 Pipe around the cassette window with red royal icing. Decorate with black royal icing.

7 Make the headset from liquorice catherine wheels, red liquorice laces and red fizzy lances.

STEP

2

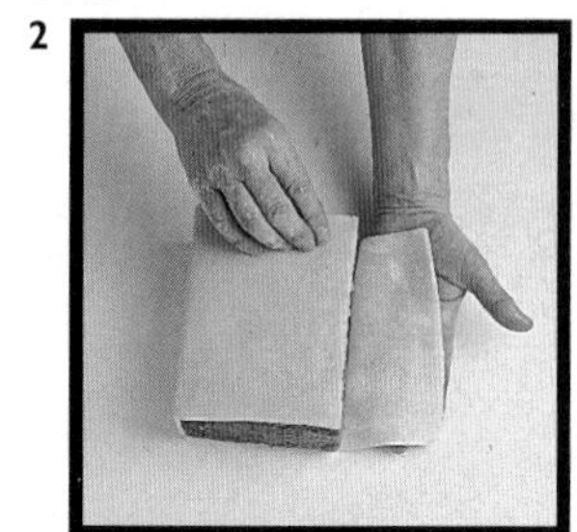

3

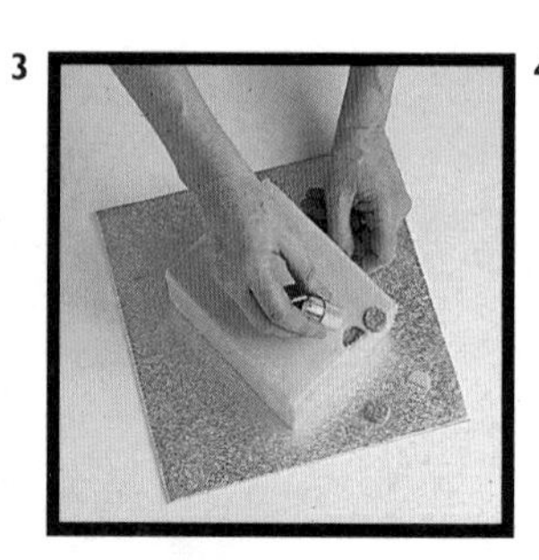

4

6

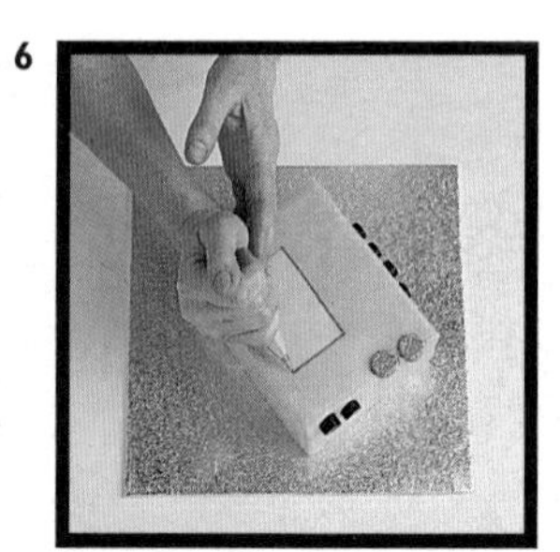

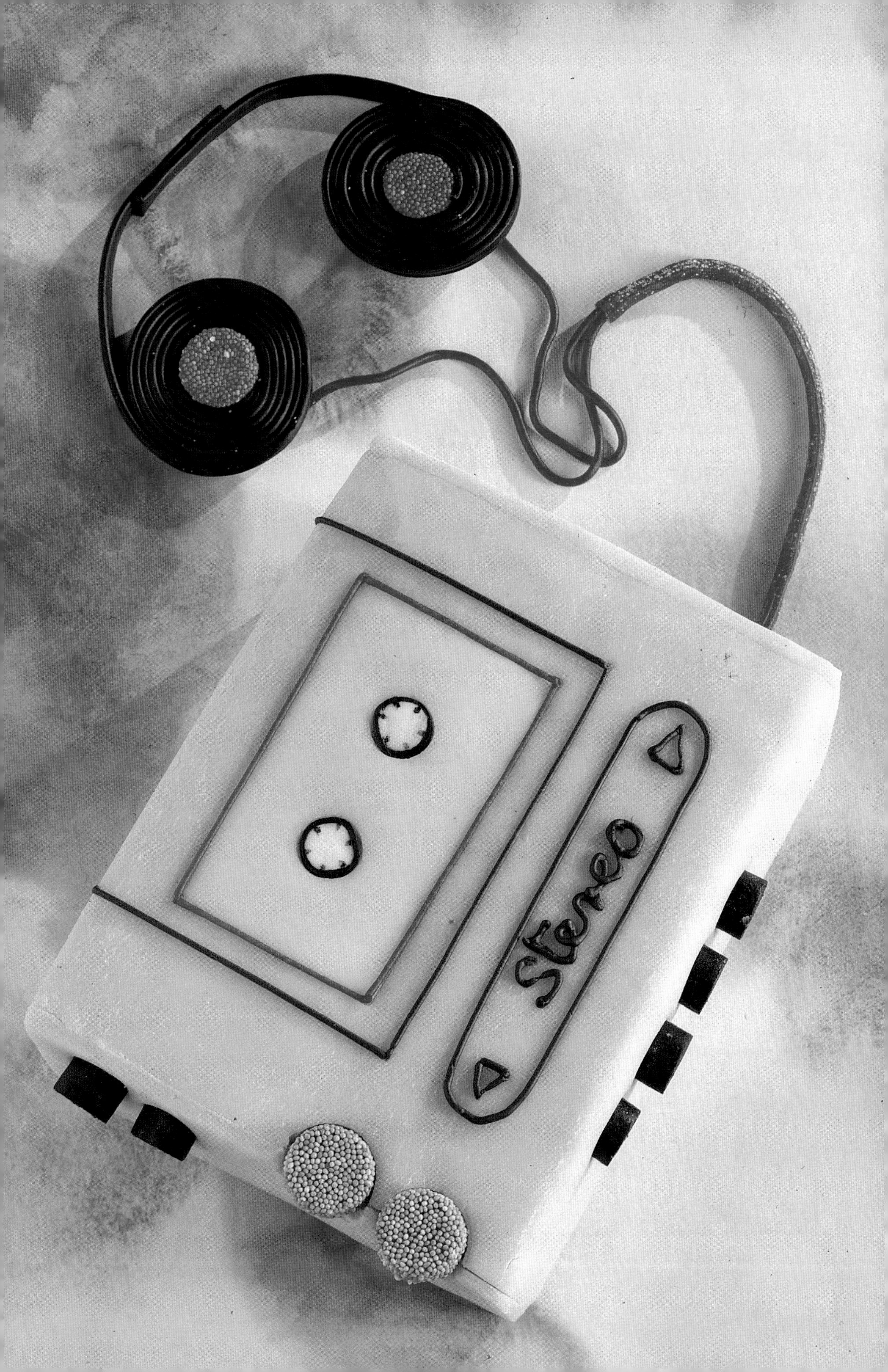
Stereo

ROSIE RABBIT

3-egg Victoria sandwich mixture baked in a 20 cm (8 inch) sandwich tin, 12.5 cm (5 inch) round tin and two 8 cm (3¼ inch) barquette moulds

225 g (8 oz) pink butter icing

sponge fingers

desiccated coconut

1 pink marshmallow

1 brown chocolate bean

2 round white mints

spaghetti

pink liquorice allsorts

1 Cut both cakes in half as shown. Sandwich the two halves of the larger cake with pink butter icing. Stand upright on a cake board.

2 Sandwich the smaller cake, cut as shown for the head and place in position on the cake board.

3 Separate the offcut, cut one piece in half as shown, then shape to resemble haunches. Cut sponge fingers to shape for legs.

4 Assemble the rabbit as shown, using the barquette shapes as ears. Cut the nose to shape.

5 Coat the cake with pink butter icing and sprinkle with desiccated coconut. Coat the barquette ears with pink butter icing and sprinkle desiccated coconut on the rounded side only. Place the ears in position.

6 Stick the marshmallow tail, chocolate bean nose and white mint eyes in position with a dab of pink icing. Push the spaghetti whiskers in place.

7 Cut two thin pink slices from liquorice allsorts and make small cuts along one side. Bend into a curve and stick above the eyes with a dab of icing. Paint in a pupil on the eyes, if liked. Add two sweet teeth as well.

STEP

1

2

3

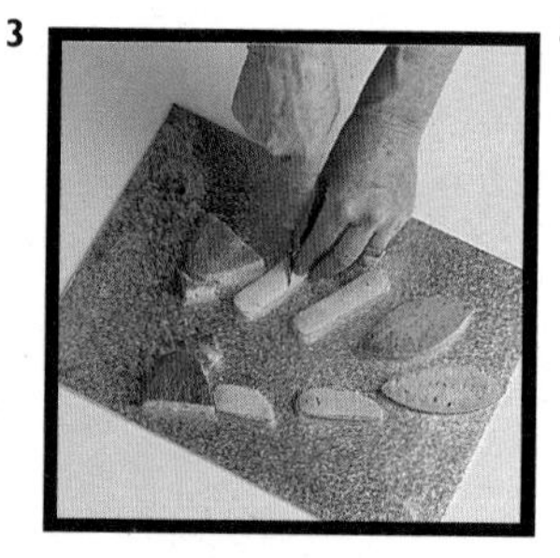

4

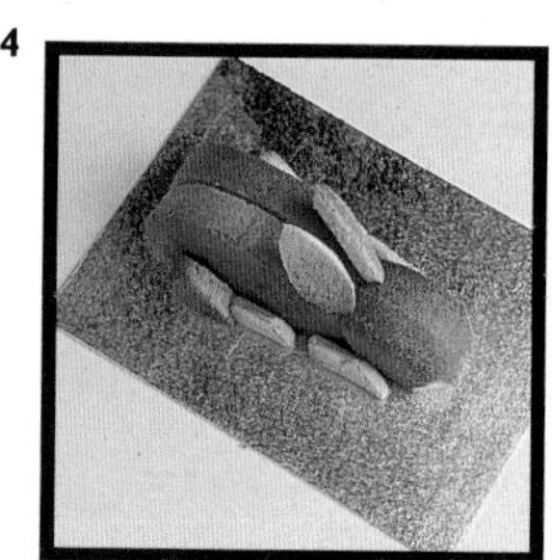

TOMMY TURTLE

5-egg Madeira cake mixture baked in a 4 litre (7 pint) basin and an 18 cm (7 inch) shallow square tin
•
apricot glaze
•
25 g (1 oz) melted chocolate
•
5 sponge fingers
•
100 g (4 oz) yellow butter icing
•
450 g (1 lb) green moulding icing
•
100 g (4 oz) yellow royal icing
•
50 g (2 oz) green royal icing
•
red liquorice
•
black liquorice
•
2 chocolate beans
•
chopped blue jelly
•
brown sugar

1 Cut a small circle from the edge of the basin cake for the head to fit into, then brush the cake with apricot glaze.

2 Cut a 4 cm (1½ inch) strip from two sides of the square cake, as shown.

3 Cut the remaining strips of sponge to a head. Shape and stick together with melted chocolate. Cut the sponge fingers to form a tail and legs, then stick together with melted chocolate.

4 Lay the cut square cake on a cake board, spread with a little yellow butter icing and lay the basin cake on top. Press the cakes gently together. Coat the head, tail and legs with yellow butter icing and place in position, supporting the head with an offcut wedge of sponge.

5 Roll out the green moulding icing into a 28 cm (11 inch) round and use to cover the glazed cake. Trim off excess icing with scissors, leaving a 1 cm (½ inch) overlap, and ease the icing into the neck area and under the body.

6 Pipe yellow royal icing on the shell to resemble the markings on a shell. Pipe green royal icing on the head.

7 Cut red liquorice into strips for claws and a piece of black liquorice for the mouth. Attach two chocolate beans for the eyes. Put the blue jelly on one side of the board and brown sugar on the other to resemble sea and sand.

STEP

1

2

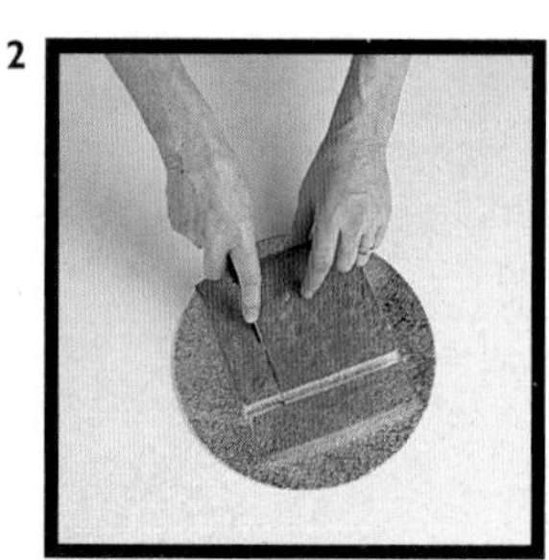

3

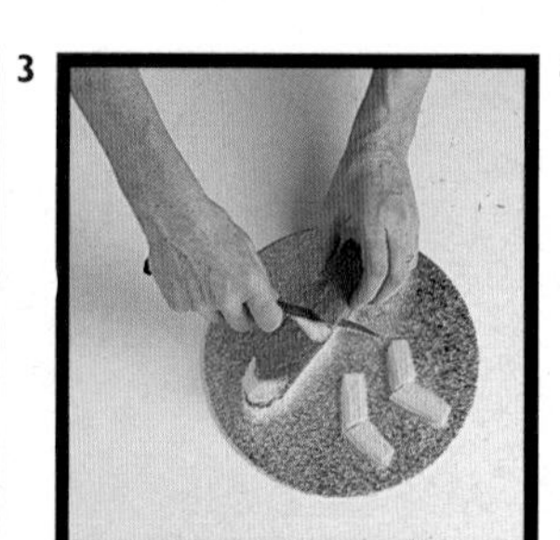

4

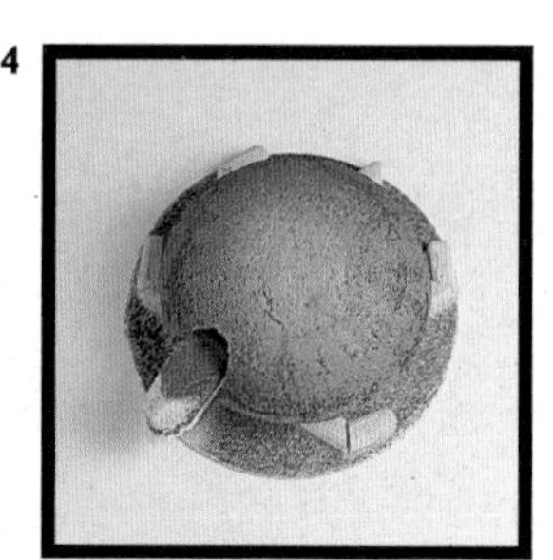

CONCORDE

225 g (8 oz) melted white chocolate
•
wafers
•
4 oblong chocolate finger wafers
•
4 mini chocolate coated Swiss rolls
•
50 g (2 oz) melted chocolate
•
ice cream cones
•
2 chocolate finger biscuits
•
3 candy sticks
•
3 chocolate buttons
•
6 Minstrels
•
egg white
•
700 g (1½ lb) white moulding icing
•
liquorice allsorts
•
50 g (2 oz) red royal icing

1 Draw a template on greaseproof paper and spread with melted white chocolate. Press the wafers into position horizontally as shown. Spread melted white chocolate evenly over the wafers and immediately cover with a second layer of wafers in the opposite direction, ensuring that the wafers overlap on every join. Spread the top with more chocolate and leave to dry.
2 Lay a template on top and with a sharp knife saw to shape with a vertical cutting action. Remove all paper.
3 Using melted chocolate, stick four chocolate finger wafer biscuits to the wings to resemble engines and leave to set.
4 Stick four mini Swiss rolls together with melted chocolate to make the fuselage and allow to dry. Shape the cones for the nose and tail. Put a chocolate finger biscuit inside each cone and stick in position. When set, attach to each end of the fuselage, using the biscuit to stick into the Swiss rolls.
5 Stick three candy sticks on to chocolate buttons with melted chocolate. Place two minstrels on either side of the candy stick for wheels.
6 Brush the top and sides of the wafer wings with egg white. Roll out white moulding icing thinly, cut to shape and cover wings, easing icing over the sides.
7 Lay the fuselage in position on the wings. Roll out moulding icing to a rectangle measuring 40.5 × 9 cm (16 × 3½ inches); drape over the fuselage, trim off any excess and mould into the wings. Where the nose and tail overlap the wings, wrap the icing underneath. Pull out to a point at the nose and tail.
8 Cut liquorice allsorts and stick in place. Cut a tail fin from wafer, coat in white chocolate and attach. Decorate with red royal icing. Position the undercarriage with Concorde on top.

STEP

1

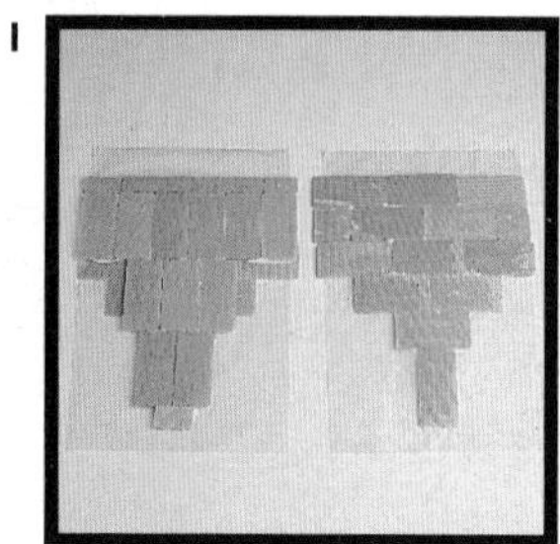

2

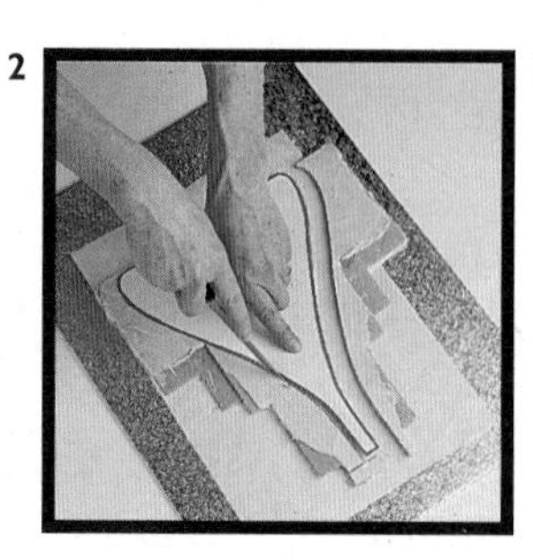

3

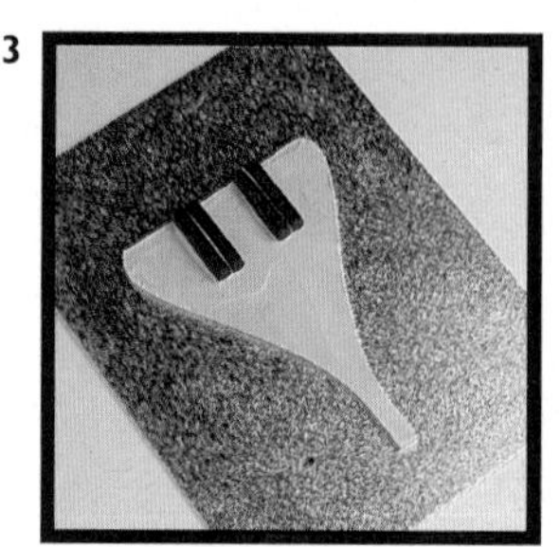

4

SANDCASTLE

4-egg Madeira cake mixture baked in a 1 litre (2 pint) flower pot and 3 dariole moulds
•
apricot glaze
•
450 g (1 lb) marzipan
•
fine demerara sugar
•
chocolate thin mint crisps
•
100 g (4 oz) yellow butter icing
•
lollipops
•
chocolate beans
•
candy sticks
•
mini liquorice allsorts
•
liquorice comfits
•
wafers

1 Trim the tops of the cakes to make level, then brush all over with apricot glaze.

2 Roll out the marzipan thinly, cut into curved strips the same height as the cakes and wrap around the sponges to coat completely. Cut rounds the same size as the small ends of the cakes. Put on the cakes and seal all joins with a palette knife.

3 Brush the cakes again, very thinly, with apricot glaze and roll in sugar to coat completely.

4 Cut the chocolate thin crisps into window and door shapes, then attach to cake with butter icing. Put lollipops on each castle and decorate the tops with sweets for battlements.

5 Coat the cake board with yellow butter icing. Arrange the sandcastles on the board. Sprinkle the board with sugar to look like sand.

6 Cut wafers to shape, then position and stick them between the castles. Decorate the courtyard with chocolate shells, if liked.

STEP

2

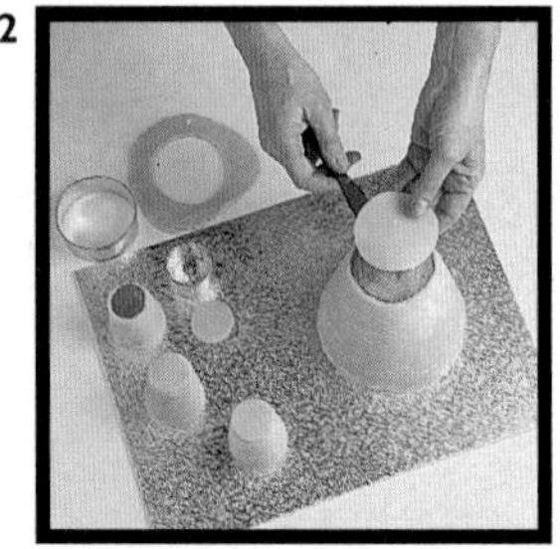

3

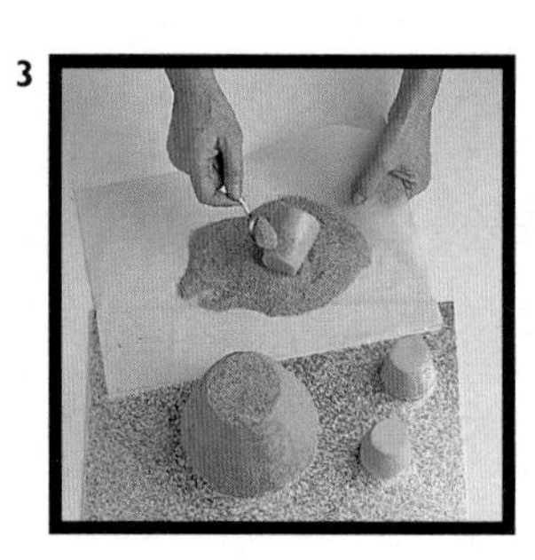

4

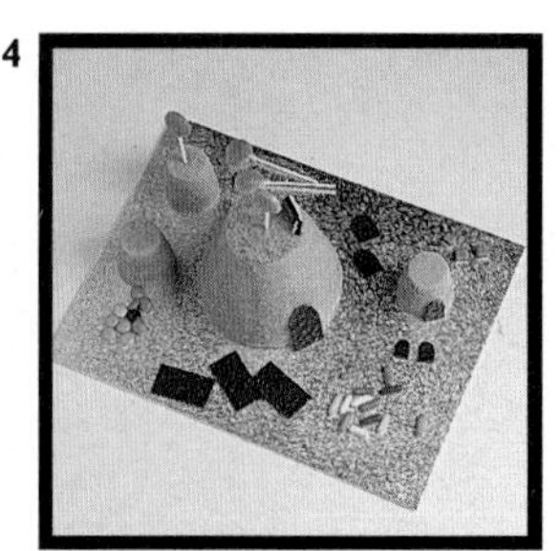

6

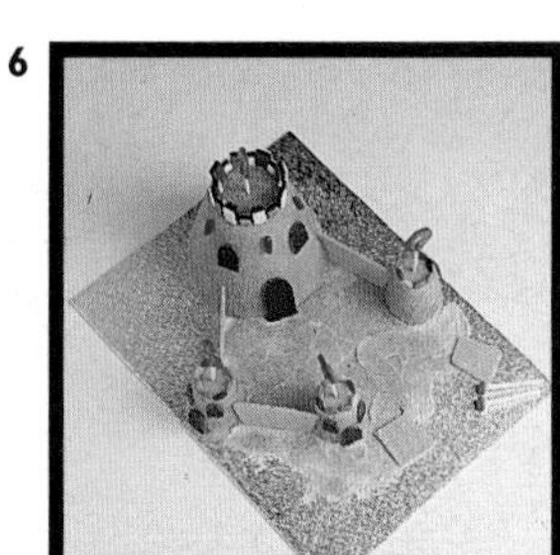

ATHLETIC TRACK

5-egg Victoria sandwich mixture baked in a 20x30 cm (8x12 inch) Swiss roll tin and 20 cm (8 inch) sandwich tin
•
225 g (8 oz) chocolate butter icing
•
225 g (8 oz) green butter icing
•
green desiccated coconut
•
100 g (4 oz) white royal icing
•
soft brown sugar
•
chocolate vermicelli or flakes
•
candy sticks
•
25 g (1 oz) white melted chocolate
•
marshmallow strip
•
plastic athletes

1 Cut the round cake in half vertically and attach half to each end of the oblong cake.
2 Cover the sides with chocolate butter icing. Spread chocolate butter icing on top of the cake around the edge and smooth evenly to form the track. Spread green butter icing in the centre and sprinkle green coconut on top.
3 Pipe white lines around the running track, using white royal icing as shown.
4 Using a teaspoon and a knife, remove some green icing in order to make a high jump and long jump track and a discus pad. Insert sugar and chocolate vermicelli as shown.
5 Make a high jump and landing mat with candy sticks, melted white chocolate and a marshmallow strip as shown. Place the athlete figures in position on the track.

STEP

1
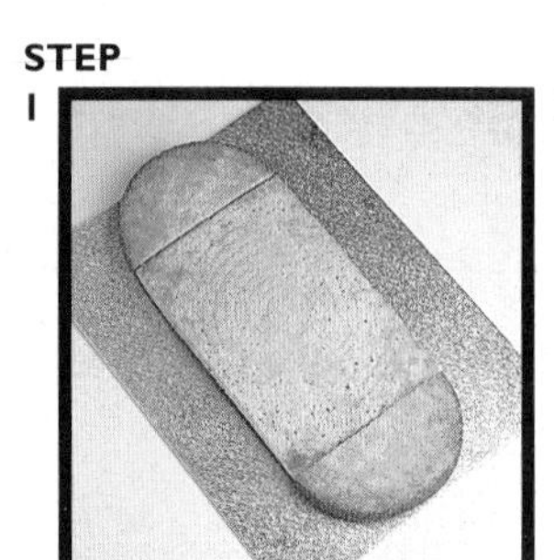

3
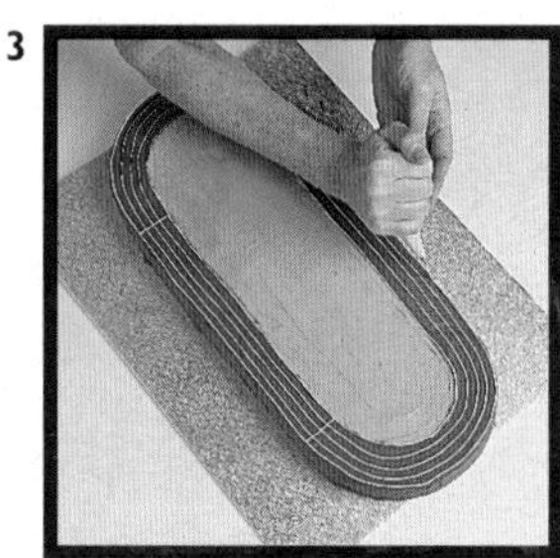

4
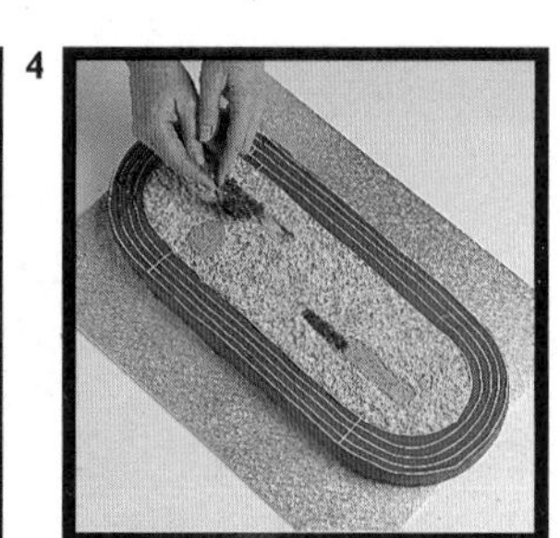

5
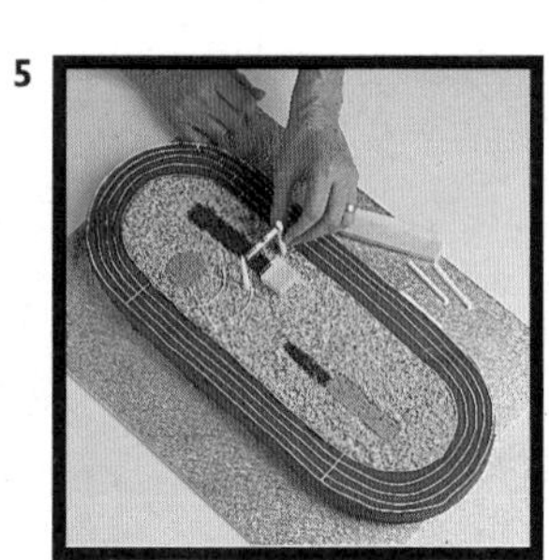

SAILING BOAT

3-egg Madeira cake mixture baked in two 450 g (1 lb) loaf tins
•
100 g (4 oz) vanilla butter icing
•
wafers
•
100 g (4 oz) green butter icing
•
50 g (2 oz) red royal icing
•
liquorice allsorts
•
Matchmakers
•
25 g (1 oz) melted chocolate
•
rice paper
•
liquorice laces
•
2 chocolate beans
•
1 candy stick
•
1 chocolate thin mint crisp

1 From one cake, cut the bow to shape with an angled cut as shown.

2 Cut the other cake in half vertically and shape the stern with an angled cut as shown. Cut the remaining piece of cake in half horizontally.

3 Cut a 2.5 cm (1 inch) strip from the centre of the bottom piece of cake and discard the centre strip. Stick the two outer pieces together to form the cabin and stick on top of the boat. Shape the forward hatch from the remaining cake.

4 Ice the cabin with vanilla butter icing and put a wafer square on the hatch.

5 Cover the sides and top deck with green butter icing and smooth evenly. Cut wafers into thin strips and position on top for the decking.

6 Pipe red royal icing around the edges of the cabin and wafer, and top of the hull. Put liquorice allsort portholes in position.

7 Stick two Matchmakers together end to end with melted chocolate and leave to set. Cut out sails from rice paper. Dot the edge of the main sail with chocolate and press the long Matchmaker in position. Stick the boom on the bottom of the sail with chocolate and butt up to the mast, sticking with chocolate.

8 Make a hole in the cabin roof for the mast. Insert the Matchmaker and sail in position on the cake.

9 Melt the end of the liquorice lace (see page 10) and press together firmly to form a small loop.

10 Place the liquorice loop from the top of the mast to the bow and fix with icing and a chocolate bean. Put an anchor cut from liquorice on the deck. Put liquorice lace hand rails on the cabin. Make a tiller from a candy stick and a rudder from a chocolate thin mint crisp.

STEP

1

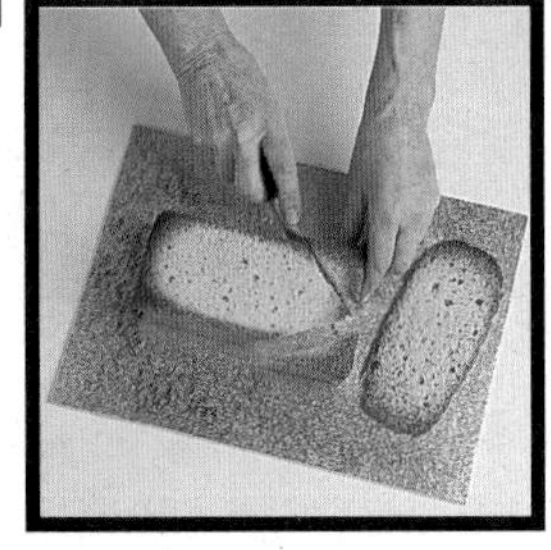

2

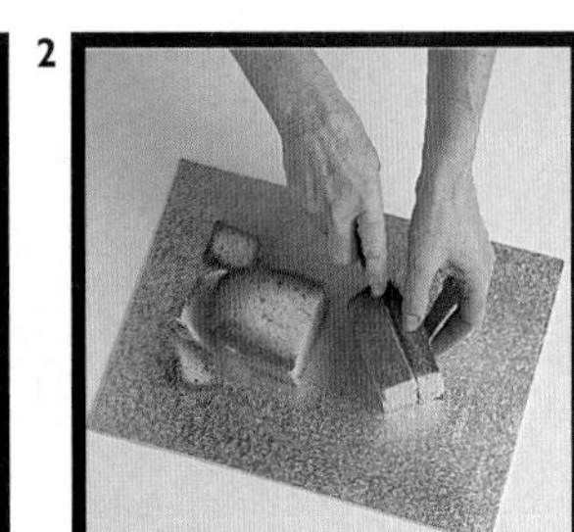

3

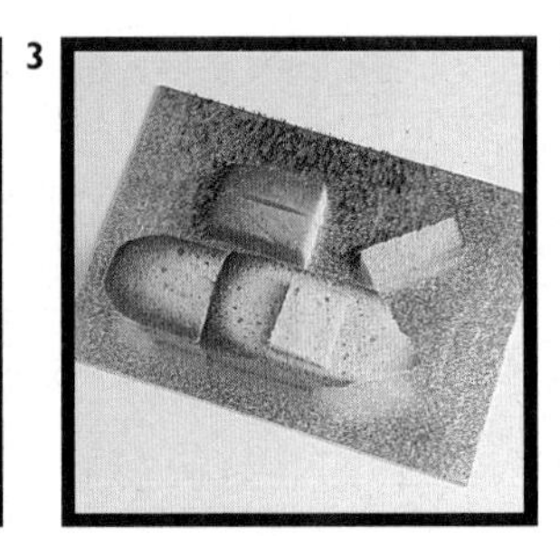

7

DISCO CAKE

3-egg Victoria sandwich cooked in 20 × 30 cm (8 × 12 inch) Swiss roll tin
•
apricot glaze
•
175 g (6 oz) pink moulding icing
•
175 g (6 oz) red moulding icing
•
175 g (6 oz) mauve moulding icing
•
100 g (4 oz) blue moulding icing
•
100 g (4 oz) green moulding icing
•
chocolate beans
•
5 sandwich wafer biscuits
•
225 g (8 oz) melted chocolate
•
50 g (2 oz) red moulding icing
•
liquorice allsorts
•
liquorice comfits
•
wafers
•
2 chocolate coated mini Swiss rolls
•
2 mini Mars bars or similar
•
red royal icing

1 Cut triangular templates for the desired design. Brush the cake with apricot glaze. Roll out the coloured moulding icings and, using the templates, cut triangles of colours and lay them on the cake. Mould the joins together with the fingers dipped in icing sugar. Trim off excess icing at the base.

2 Use a small cutter or end of a plain piping nozzle, cut 1 cm (½ inch) rounds from the icing and ease out with the point of a knife. Drop chocolate beans into the holes and gently press into position.

3 Cut one wafer biscuit to shape as shown and stick the wafers together with melted chocolate.

4 Coat the wafer construction with melted chocolate and leave to dry. Stick a small piece of red moulding icing on top of the deck. Add liquorice allsorts as turntables. Stick chocolate beans on the front with melted chocolate and decorate with liquorice comfits.

5 To make the speakers, cut wafers to size and stick to the backs of the mini Swiss rolls with melted chocolate. Cut three-quarters from two mini Mars bars and stick wafers on the back with melted chocolate. Leave to dry. Pipe around the wafers with red royal icing and stick to the top of the mini Swiss rolls with melted chocolate.

6 Stick the speakers in position on the dance floor and decorate with more sweets and piping as liked.

STEP

2
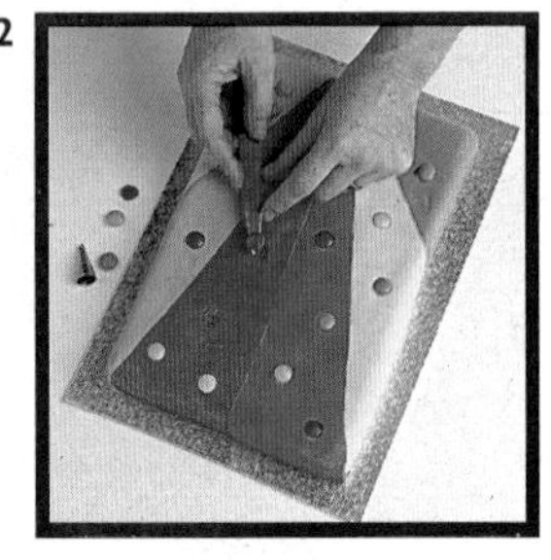

3

4

5

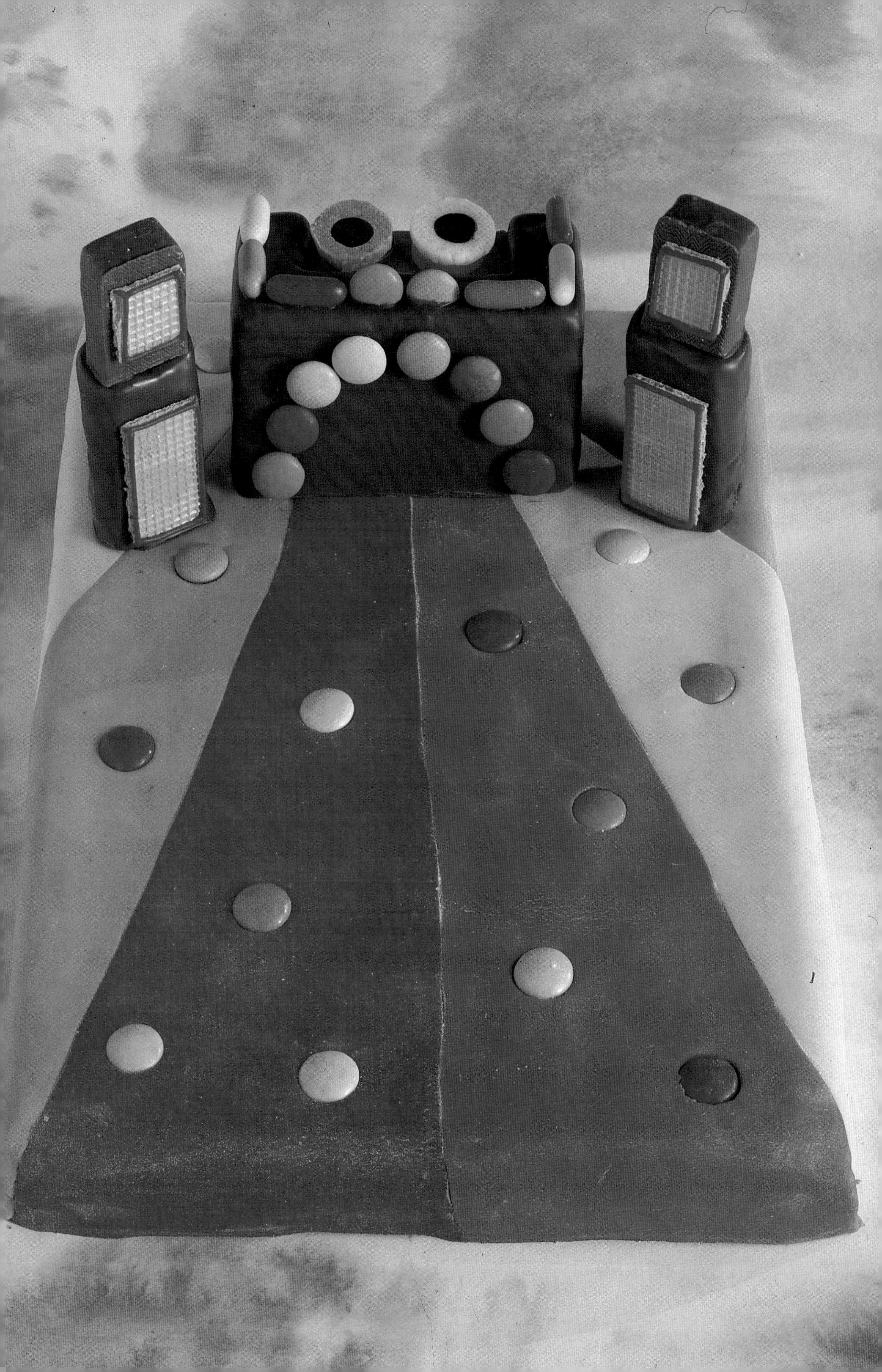

SWIMMING POOL

1 Cut the pool shape from one of the cakes, using the template, and reserve the sponge for rocks and bushes.
2 Sandwich the cakes together with green butter icing and cut away a portion of the top cake to make a step. Brush apricot glaze over the sides and base of the pool. Cut the dariole mould cake in half to form bushes and attach to the cake with green butter icing. Cut the offcut piece of sponge into rocks and bushes.
3 Roll out the blue moulding icing, using the template cut out the pool shape and position in the base of the pool. Cut a long 1 cm (½ inch) wide strip of moulding icing and place up the side of the pool.

6-egg Victoria sandwich mixture baked in two 20 × 30 cm (8 × 12 inch) Swiss roll tins lined to extend 2.5 cm (1 inch) above edge of tin and 1 dariole mould
•
100 g (4 oz) green butter icing
•
apricot glaze
•
100 g (4 oz) blue moulding icing
•
50 g (2 oz) chocolate butter icing
•
chocolate thin mint crisps
•
sandwich wafer biscuits
•
green desiccated coconut
•
wafers
•
Polos
•
liquorice allsorts
•
edible flowers
•
50 g (2 oz) red royal icing
•
blue piping gel or chopped blue jelly

4 Cover the bushes and top and sides of the cake with green butter icing. Cover the rocks with chocolate butter icing. Place the bushes and rocks in position.
5 Cut chocolate thin crisps to size and place around the pool. Cut wafer biscuits into steps and place in position. Sprinkle the green icing on top of the cake with green coconut.
6 Attach wafers to the side of the cake for a fence. Attach Polos to the fence for life belts.
7 Make lilos from liquorice allsort slices. Position edible flowers and pipe red dots on the bushes.
8 Fill the pool with blue piping gel or chopped jelly, then float a lilo on top. Add other decorations as liked.

STEP
1

2
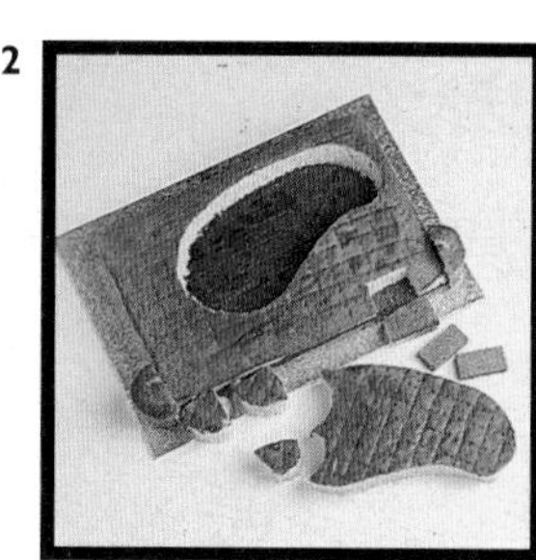

3
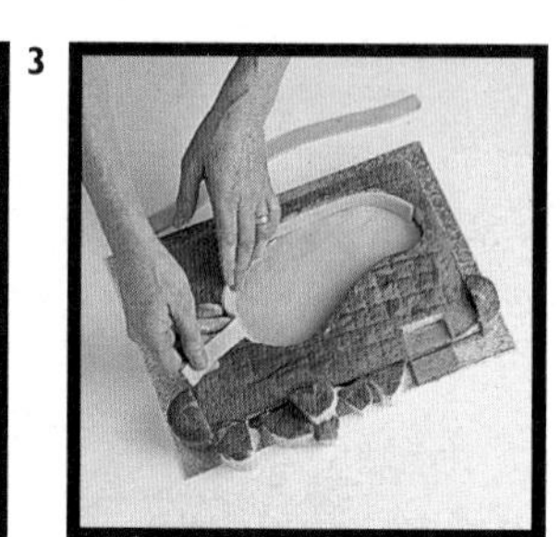

5

GUITAR

6-egg Victoria sandwich mixture baked in two 20 × 30 cm (8 × 12 inch) Swiss roll tins lined to extend 2.5 cm (1 inch) above edge of tin
•
225 g (8 oz) chocolate butter icing
•
apricot glaze
•
350 g (12 oz) brown marzipan
•
brown food colouring
•
5 mini chocolate coated Swiss rolls
•
1 chocolate Swiss roll
•
chocolate thin mint crisps
•
100 g (4 oz) red royal icing
•
liquorice comfits
•
100 g (4 oz) white royal icing
•
chocolate decorations (optional)

1 Sandwich the cakes together with chocolate butter icing. Cut to shape as shown with the help of a template, if preferred. Brush the top with apricot glaze.
2 Spread chocolate butter icing over the sides of the cake and smooth evenly.
3 Roll out the brown marzipan, cut roughly to shape and lay over the top of the cake. Trim off any excess icing with a sharp knife.
4 Using a plain cutter, mark a circle in the middle as shown. Paint with brown food colouring. Put the guitar on a cake board.
5 Lay four mini Swiss rolls in position on the board. Cut the large Swiss roll in half horizontally and stick on top of mini Swiss rolls with icing. Coat with chocolate butter icing.
6 Lay a mini Swiss roll at the top of the finger board to form a scroll.
7 Lay chocolate thin crisps down the length of the finger board, the last two being laid on the marzipan. Pipe frets across using red royal icing.
8 Insert red liquorice comfits to form the tuning screws of the guitar.
9 Pipe red royal icing in lines and dots to decorate. Pipe white lines down the length of the guitar for the strings. Attach a Matchmaker and bought chocolate decorations, if liked.

STEP 1

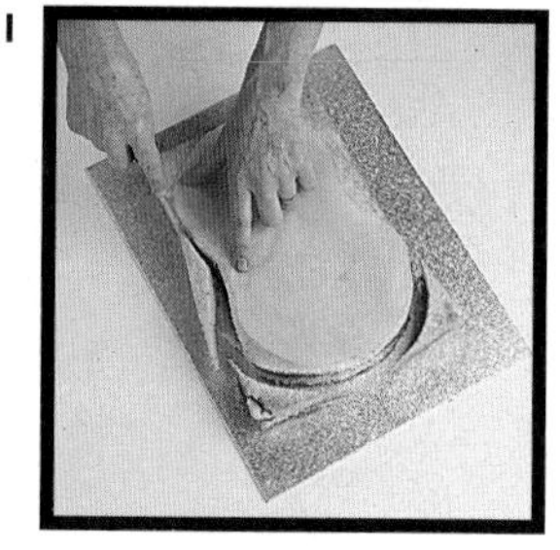

4

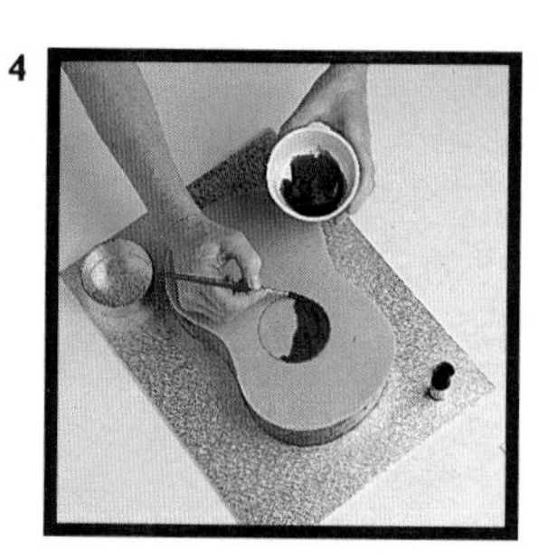

5

7

STEAM ROLLER

2 chocolate coated Swiss rolls
•
3 iced ring biscuits
•
1 bought oblong chocolate Madeira cake
•
wafers
•
long Matchmakers
•
50 g (2 oz) melted chocolate
•
1 mini chocolate coated Swiss roll
•
50 g (2 oz) melted white chocolate
•
2 Wagon Wheels
•
100 g (4 oz) yellow royal icing
•
chocolate beans
•
liquorice comfits
•
flying saucer

1 Cut two-thirds from one Swiss roll and place a biscuit on top to form the roller and swivel. Place on a cake board.

2 Cut the Madeira cake so that the height is equal to the roller height. Stand the smaller piece in position on its cut surface. Place two wafers on top, then position the Swiss roll boiler on top.

3 Position the other piece of Madeira cake, cut face down, with the flat side butting on to the boiler. Stick a biscuit wheel on each side of the boiler with icing.

4 Cut a Matchmaker in half and attach to the Swiss roll with melted chocolate half way along the length on either side for supports. Stick Matchmakers to rest on the cab roof and supports using melted chocolate.

5 Stick the mini Swiss roll in position with melted chocolate for the funnel. Spread melted chocolate on the exposed ends of the Swiss rolls.

6 To make the canopy, lay three wafers side by side. Lay a fourth wafer across the joins as shown, sticking with melted white chocolate. Cut 0.5 cm (¼ inch) strips of wafer and attach to three edges with melted white chocolate and leave to dry. Lay the canopy on top of the supports.

7 Attach two Wagon Wheels to the Madeira cake using melted chocolate, for the rear wheels. Cut wafers for the cab door. Pipe yellow royal icing along the boiler, cab, wheels and canopy. Attach chocolate beans in position on the wheels, liquorice comfits for lights and half a flying saucer on the front of the boiler.

Note: For a more professional finish, coat the Madeira cake with melted chocolate (see page 64). Leave to dry on greaseproof paper, then trim off the excess. Add cotton woool smoke to the funnel.

STEP

2

3

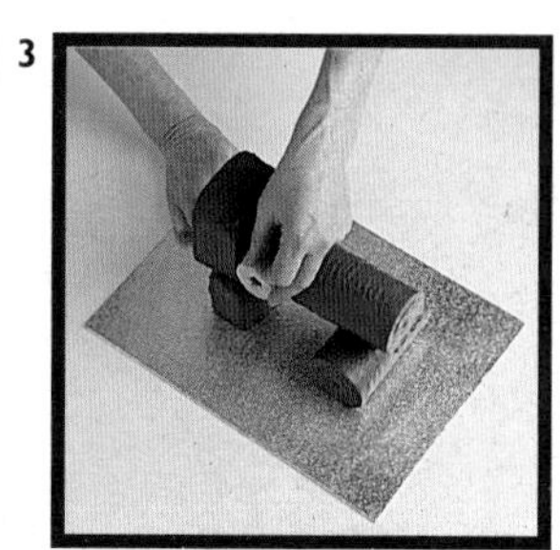

4

6

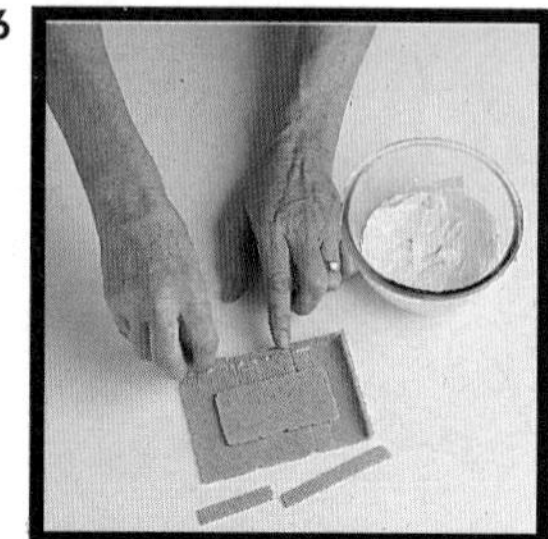

NOAH'S ARK

6-egg Madeira cake mixture baked in a 900 g (2 lb) loaf tin, 450 g (1 lb) loaf tin and 600 ml (1 pint) basin
•
100 g (4 oz) yellow butter icing
•
225 g (8 oz) red butter icing
•
wafers
•
chocolate thin mint crisps
•
50 g (2 oz) red royal icing
•
chocolate beans
•
liquorice allsorts
•
cotton wool
•
chopped blue jelly
•
animal figures

1 For the hull of the ark, trim the ends from the large loaf cake.
2 Cut the basin cake in half vertically and stick to either end of the loaf cake with icing as shown. Trim any protruding cake to neaten the shape.
3 Cut the small loaf cake, shaping the roof as shown. Coat the cake with yellow butter icing, smooth evenly and place on top of the hull.
4 Coat the hull with red butter icing, smoothing evenly with a palette knife. Put the ark on a cake board.
5 Cut wafers into strips and stick on to the deck.
6 Lay the chocolate mint crisps on the roof.
7 Pipe red royal icing around the hull and elsewhere as liked.
8 Position the chocolate beans to represent the portholes, a liquorice sweet for the chimney, cotton wool for smoke and a wafer for the ladder. Add chocolate mint crisp doors. Surround with chopped blue jelly for the sea. Add animal figures.

STEP

1

2
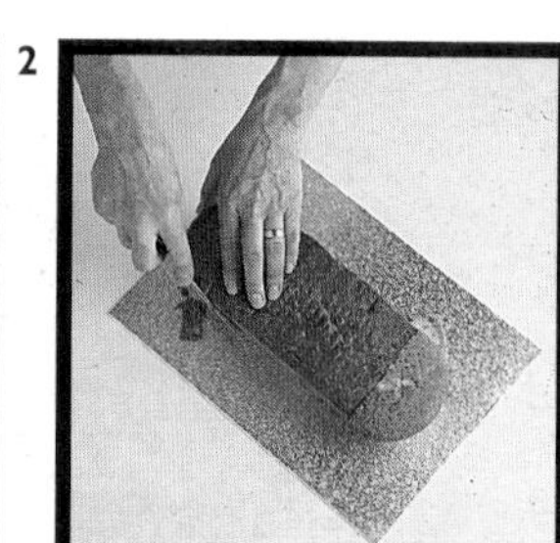

3

5

SNOOKER TABLE

5-egg Victoria sandwich mixture baked in an 18 × 28 cm (7 × 11 inch) tin and 20 × 30 cm (8 × 12 inch) Swiss roll tin
•
225 g (8 oz) chocolate butter icing
•
apricot glaze
•
400 g (14 oz) green marzipan
•
6 liquorice allsorts
•
egg white
•
50 g (2 oz) brown moulding icing
•
50 g (2 oz) marzipan
•
red, black, brown, yellow and blue food colourings
•
50 g (2 oz) white royal icing

1 Using a 0.5 cm (¼ inch) cutter, remove small rounds of cake as shown from the larger cake.
2 Sandwich the two cakes together with chocolate butter icing putting the larger cake on top, underside up. Spread chocolate butter icing over the sides of both cakes.
3 Brush the top of the cake with apricot glaze. Roll out the green marzipan, cut to size and lay over the top. Remove small circles of marzipan over the pockets.
4 Using a little icing, position liquorice allsorts in the holes.
5 Roll out the remaining green marzipan into a long strip 0.5 cm (¼ inch) thick. Cut out six 18 cm (7 inch) lengths, 0.5 cm (¼ inch) wide. Brush the top edges of the cake with egg white and stick the strips into place along the edges.
6 Mould two cues from brown moulding icing and leave to dry. If liked, mould a little white moulding icing at the end of each cue or coat the ends with a little white royal icing. Shape six 3 mm (⅛ inch) rolls of brown moulding icing and fit around the liquorice allsorts to form the pocket tops. Using plain marzipan and appropriate food colouring, mould 15 red balls, and one white, black, pink, blue, green, brown and yellow ball. Leave to dry.
7 Pipe white lines on the table with royal icing. Position the balls and cues on the table.

STEP

1

4

5

6
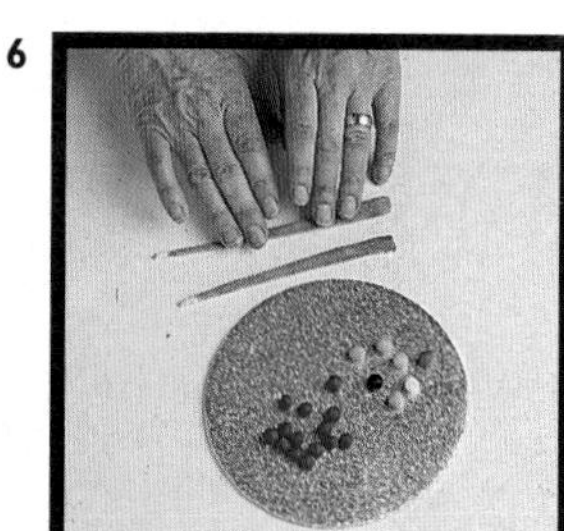

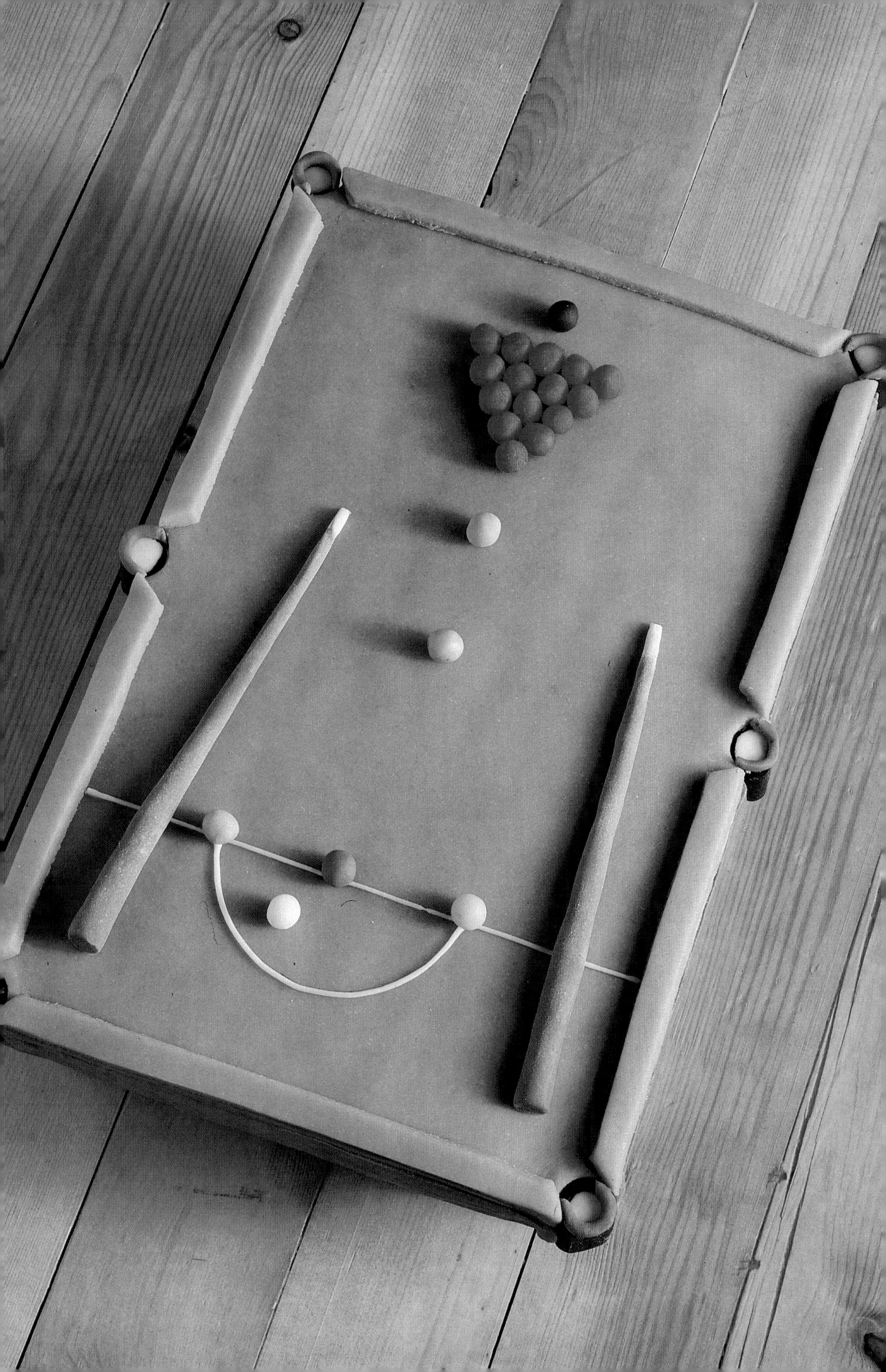

OZZIE OWL

4-egg Madeira cake mixture baked in a 600 ml (1 pint) basin and 900 ml (1 ½ pint) basin
•
225 g (8 oz) chocolate butter icing
•
liquorice allsorts
•
liquorice strip
•
50 g (2 oz) vanilla butter icing

1 Cut a slice from each side of the larger cake and cut to shape for wings.
2 Cut a slice from one side of the small cake and cut to shape for ears.
3 Assemble the cake on a cake board and stick together with chocolate butter icing.
4 Cut liquorice allsorts to shape for the feet, beak and eyes. Use pinking shears to cut eyebrows from liquorice strip.
5 Cover the assembled cake with chocolate butter icing and, using a palette knife, mark the icing to resemble feathers. Dab vanilla butter icing on the breast, wing tips and ears.
6 Smooth the icing on the face with a palette knife. Place liquorice allsort eyes, eyebrows, beak and feet into position, pressing into the icing gently.

STEP

1

2

3

5
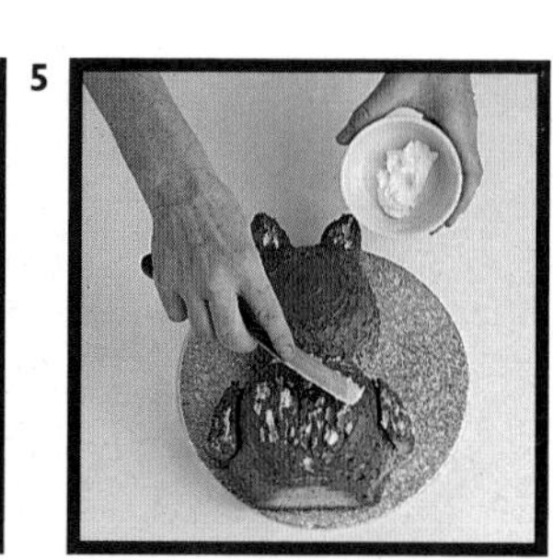

TREE STUMP

3 chocolate Swiss rolls
•
225 g (8 oz) chocolate butter icing
•
6 chocolate flakes
•
100 g (4 oz) coffee butter icing
•
50 g (2 oz) melted chocolate
•
bought ladybirds and creepy crawlies
•
1 fabric robin
•
50 g (2 oz) green butter icing

1 Cut the three Swiss rolls as shown.
2 Stand four pieces upright on a cake board so that the short and long sides meet to form a slope. Cut one of the half Swiss rolls into half lengthways. Assemble on either side of the tree stump, sticking together with chocolate butter icing.
3 Cut the remaining half into lengths to fill the central gap.
4 Coat the sides with chocolate butter icing. Cut the flakes in half lengthways and across. Stick them around the sides of the cake.
5 Cover the top with coffee butter icing and use a fork to mark into circles. Carefully mark rings in the wood around the top, using melted chocolate and a knife.
6 Add ladybirds and creepy crawlies as desired and put the robin in position. Cover the cake board with green butter icing, roughing up with a palette knife.

STEP

1
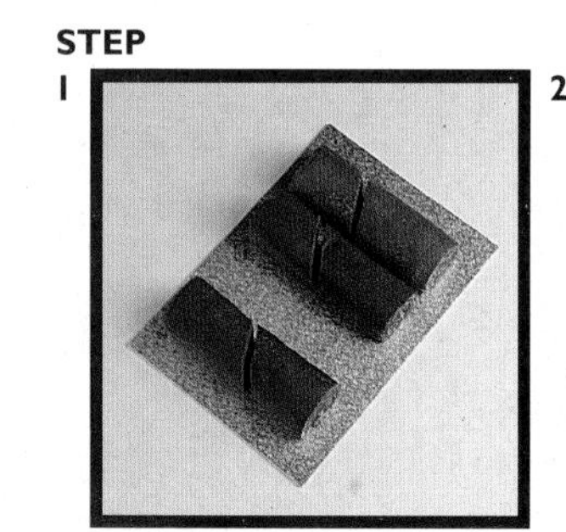

2

4

5

SID SNAIL

4-egg Victoria sandwich mixture baked in a 1 litre (2 pint) basin, 18 cm (7 inch) shallow square tin and 1 cup cake
•
225 g (8 oz) red butter icing
•
apricot glaze
•
225 g (8 oz) yellow moulding icing
•
chocolate beans
•
2 lollipops

1 Cut the square cake as shown, levelling the top of the cake, if necessary.
2 Stick the two long pieces together with red butter icing and cut both ends to shape as shown.
3 Build the head from the small pieces of cake and cut to shape. Fill up any gaps and stick together with butter icing.
4 Stick the cup cake to the top of the basin cake with butter icing and trim to a smooth shape for the shell.
5 Brush the head and body with apricot glaze. Roll out the yellow moulding icing to an oblong shape and lift on to the cake, moulding it to shape. Trim off any excess icing.
6 Spread the shell of the snail with the red butter icing and use a palette knife to carefully swirl the icing into a spiral pattern.
7 Stick chocolate beans on the shell in a spiral pattern.
8 Stick eyes on to the head with a little icing, pipe a mouth and attach two lollipops for antennae. If liked, make a path with chocolate thin mint crisps and grass from green desiccated coconut.

STEP

1

2
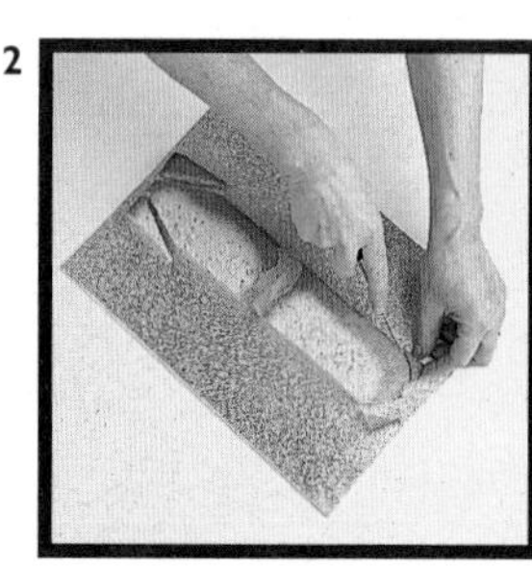

3
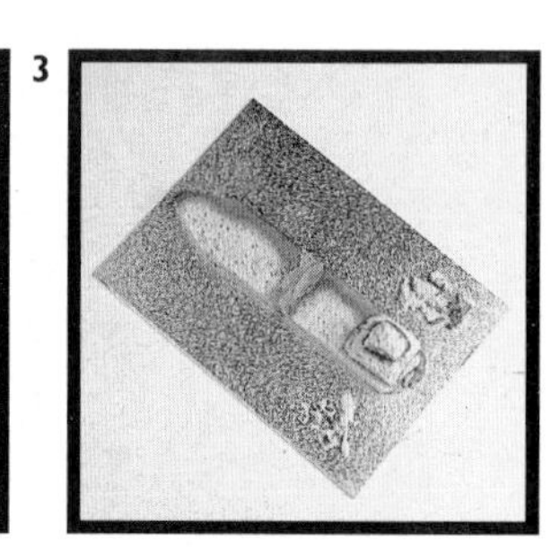

4

RIDGE TENT

3 bought oblong Madeira cakes
•
100 g (4 oz) butter icing
•
apricot glaze
•
700 g (1½ lb) orange marzipan
•
red food colouring
•
egg white
•
Matchmakers
•
red liquorice laces
•
angelica (optional)
•
100 g (4 oz) red royal icing

1 Cut one Madeira cake diagonally in half as shown, then stand the halves on the two narrowest sides.

2 Lay the two remaining cakes side by side on their sides, rounded tops inward. Lay the cut cake in position across the top in the opposite direction.

3 Trim the cakes to the shape of a tent by making diagonal cuts in the bottom cakes as shown to within 2.5 cm (1 inch) of the base. Insert the offcuts into the gaps between each side of the bottom cakes.

4 Sandwich all the cakes together with butter icing, then brush with apricot glaze.

5 Make a template of the shape of one end of the tent. Roll out half the marzipan thinly and, using the template, cut out two shapes and stick one to each end of the tent. Paint one end with red food colouring.

6 Roll out the remaining marzipan plus trimmings to a rectangle measuring 33 × 16 cm (13 × 6½ inches). Cut two lengths 2.5 cm (1 inch) wide from the shorter side and press into position along the base of each side of the tent. Carefully lay the rest of the marzipan across the ridge of the tent. Press gently into position, leaving the ends that overlap the base marzipan free.

7 Roll out the marzipan trimmings and cut out a further triangular end piece to the shape of the template. Cut in half as shown, and attach to the red painted end of the tent with egg white, pressing firmly at the diagonal edges.

8 Gently roll the inside edges back to make the tent flaps. Hold in position with food colouring bottles until set.

9 Attach a Matchmaker on the red painted end for a ridge pole. Insert small pieces of Matchmaker at each end of the tent ridge, making a hole with a 0.5 cm (¼ inch) skewer first. Attach red liquorice guy ropes and fix to the ground with Matchmaker or angelica tent pegs. Pipe more tent pegs along the side edges of the tent with red royal icing and decorate as liked.

STEP

1

2

3

8

PADDOCK

4-egg Victoria sandwich mixture baked in a 20 × 30 cm (8 × 12 inch) Swiss roll tin
•
100 g (4 oz) chocolate butter icing
•
chocolate flakes
•
225 g (8 oz) green butter icing
•
green desiccated coconut (optional)
•
chocolate finger biscuits
•
Matchmakers
•
25 g (1 oz) melted chocolate
•
chocolate thin mint crisps
•
fudge
•
2 Rolos
•
chocolate fudge bar
•
plastic horses and trees

1 Ice the sides of the cake with chocolate butter icing and coat with chocolate flakes.
2 Ice the top of the cake with green butter icing and rough up with a palette knife or cover with green coconut.
3 Make the log shelter as shown using chocolate finger biscuits with Matchmakers, sticking with melted chocolate.
4 Attach a roof to the log shelter using chocolate thin mint crisps with Matchmakers as shown.
5 Make the fence as shown using Matchmakers and melted chocolate.
6 Cut fudge to shape and rough up with a fork to make half bales. Put two Rolos together to make a water butt. Balance the chocolate fudge bar on two small pieces of Matchmaker and stick with melted chocolate, to make a water trough.
7 Place horse figures and trees in position.

STEP

3

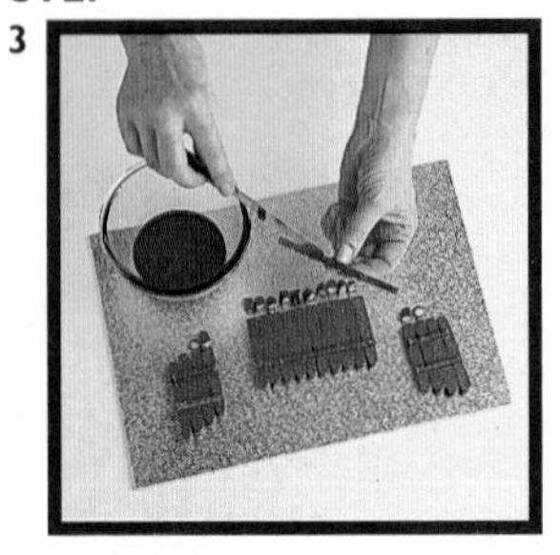

4

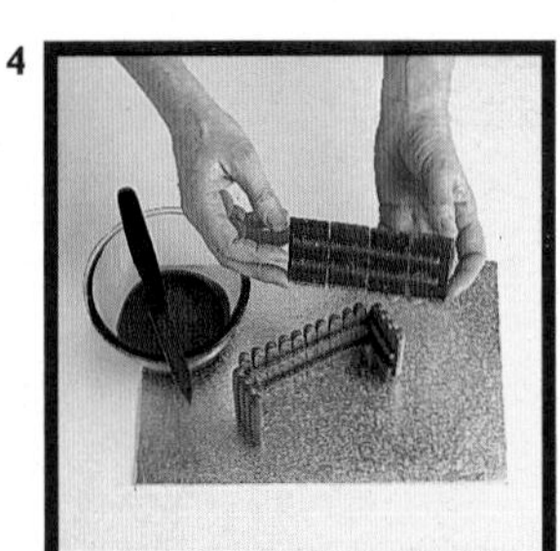

5

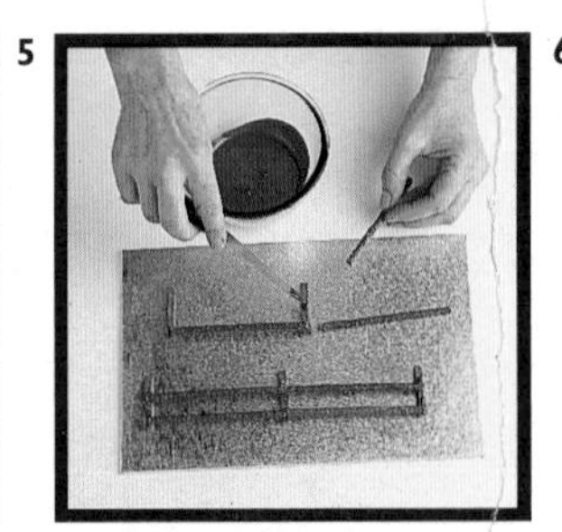

6

MARY, MARY, QUITE CONTRARY

3-egg Madeira cake mixture baked in a 1 litre (2 pint) flower pot and 1 dariole mould
•
apricot glaze
•
450 g (1 lb) blue moulding icing
•
100 g (4 oz) white moulding icing
•
egg white
•
1 pink marshmallow
•
50 g (2 oz) pink moulding icing
•
100 g (4 oz) pink royal icing
•
50 g (2 oz) brown royal icing

1 For the body, cut a small diagonal piece from the top of the dariole mould cake and a slice from the opposite side.

2 Brush both cakes with apricot glaze. Roll out a quarter of the blue moulding icing and use to coat the dariole mould bodice.

3 Roll out the white moulding icing and cut a long strip about 5 cm (2 inches) wide. Place around the bottom of the inverted flower pot cake. Make a frill (see page 52) and attach with egg white.

4 Roll out the remaining blue icing to a 24 cm (9½ inch) round. Lift over the flower pot cake and flute the bottom for her skirt.

5 Use the blue icing trimmings to cut a 6 cm (2½ inch) round and mould around the marshmallow head to make the hat. Leave to set.

6 Mould two puff sleeves from blue moulding icing trimmings and arms and hands from the pink moulding icing.

7 Attach the pink arms to the puff sleeves with egg white and leave to set. With the bodice lying flat on its back, attach the arms with royal icing and leave to set.

8 Roll a piece of pink moulding icing for the neck and attach to the marshmallow with egg white; dry.

9 Using a little royal icing, stick the bodice on to the skirt. Stick her head on with egg white and support with a cocktail stick until set.

10 Using pink royal icing, pipe decorative dots around the skirt, sleeves, bodice and hat. Pipe hair with brown royal icing using a fine nozzle. Add a white moulding icing collar, if liked.

Note: Trim the marshmallow to a face shape if liked and paint on features with a fine paint brush.

STEP 1

3

4

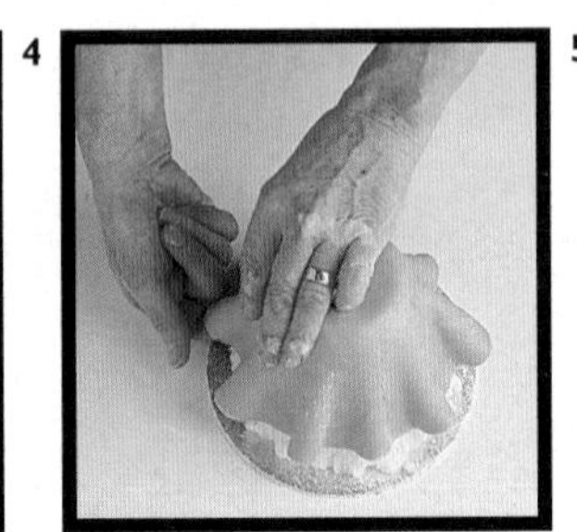

5

INDEX